# BOURBON

## — 101 —

# BOURBON

## — 101 —

ALBERT W. A. SCHMID

FOREWORD BY CHRIS MORRIS

UNIVERSITY PRESS OF KENTUCKY

*Editorial and Sales Offices:* The University Press of Kentucky
663 South Limestone Street, Lexington, Kentucky 40508-4008
www.kentuckypress.com

Library of Congress Cataloging-in-Publication Data

Names: Schmid, Albert W. A., author.
Title: Bourbon 101 / Albert W. A. Schmid ; foreword by Chris Morris.
Other titles: Bourbon one hundred one
Description: Lexington, Kentucky : The University Press of Kentucky, [2023] | Includes bibliographical references.
Identifiers: LCCN 2022060079 | ISBN 9780813197166 (hardcover) | ISBN 9780813197173 (pdf) | ISBN 9780813197180 (epub)
Subjects: LCSH: Bourbon whiskey—Kentucky.
Classification: LCC TP605 .S27 2023 | DDC 663/.5209769—dc23/eng/20221215
LC record available at https://lccn.loc.gov/2022060079

This book is printed on acid-free paper meeting
the requirements of the American National Standard
for Permanence in Paper for Printed Library Materials.

*Manufactured in the United States of America.*

Member of the Association of University Presses

*To Kendall and Thomas*


May your marriage be like a honey barrel
of bourbon, always pleasing!

# CONTENTS

# FOREWORD

Growing up in a "bourbon household" (both my parents worked at Brown-Forman Distillers), I was immersed in all things bourbon. There were, for example, three books about the industry on the living room bookshelves: *The Social History of Bourbon,* by Gerald Carson, *Bluegrass, Belles and Bourbon,* by Harry Harrison Kroll, and Brown-Forman's one hundredth anniversary celebration's *Nothing Better in the Market,* by John Ed Pearce. They spanned a period from 1964 to 1970. These three books comprised the entirety of the written word that chronicled the history of the industry as I grew up. I never would have thought that the next wave of bourbon journalism would have us waiting twenty-five years for its appearance.

Today it is easy to understand why that was the case. The bourbon industry began a decades-long decline in popularity in the late 1970s. Famous Kentucky distilleries closed and companies merged or were broken up, their brands scattered, devalued, and in many cases discontinued. My forty-six-year career began during that bleak period. It seemed that no one outside of Kentucky was interested in the story of bourbon. Vodka, wine coolers, sweet liqueurs, and wines had captured the fancy of the American consumer. Of course, we know that no trend lasts forever, and thankfully bourbon fought back, reinventing itself, and it has now returned to a position of prominence in the hearts and minds—and, more important, the glasses—of consumers across the nation.

The Bourbon Renaissance has led to a flood of new bourbon-themed books, magazines, podcasts, events, films, and more. Albert Schmid has been a prominent contributor to this phenomenon. His award-winning *The Kentucky Bourbon Cookbook* was the first of its genre to be penned by an internationally trained culinary expert. Albert admits that he originally shunned bourbon in favor of gin, so his *The Manhattan Cocktail: A Modern Guide to the Whiskey Classic* and *The Old Fashioned: An Essential Guide to the Original Whiskey Cocktail* show us all that redemption is indeed possible. Given this great body of work, it can be difficult for an author to come up with a new angle or approach. Yet Albert has done just that in *Bourbon 101*.

Albert has made the story personal by filtering it through his life experiences, such as how his father first introduced him to bourbon and how he interfaced with master distillers in his work at the Sullivan University culinary school and the International Association of Culinary Professionals. This book is the work of a true believer, not some clinician's dispassionate thesis.

*Bourbon 101* starts right out of the gate with industry definitions and leading brands identified by producer, age, proof presentation, and other basic facts. Usually, this type of information will be found at the end. But think about it—who wants to keep turning to the back of a book for information about what you are reading? Best prime the pump, so to speak, so as you go chapter by chapter you will have a good understanding of what is being presented. Each chapter ends with a quiz. How different! The quizzes are fun, easy, and sure to help you remember the material just covered. There is so much to enjoy in *Bourbon 101* that I will leave it to you for further exploration. It is time well spent on an enjoyable journey.

**CHRIS MORRIS**
MASTER DISTILLER

**Brown-Forman Distillery Company**
*(Woodford Reserve, Old Forester, King of Kentucky)*

# PREFACE

## AMERICA'S NATIVE SPIRIT

AM ALLERGIC TO CORN. SO PEOPLE WHO KNOW me well are surprised that I love bourbon because, by law, bourbon is made from at least 51% corn. Logic dictates that someone with a corn allergy should not enjoy a beverage containing so much of the offending grain. People who are allergic to gluten avoid anything made from wheat. So how did I come to learn that bourbon was safe for me to drink? I will get to that in a minute. Right now, you need to know that in my opinion, there is nothing better at the end of a long day than a glass of America's native spirit, with or without a little ice. Plus, some of the world's best cocktails, the Old Fashioned and the Manhattan, can be made with bourbon brilliantly. I may be a little biased on both of these cocktails, having written books on both, but I stand by my assessment.

I did not always hold the view that bourbon is a superior spirit. I enjoy flavor in my spirits, but I definitely did not want to end up sick after drinking a single cocktail. When I did drink whiskey, I preferred the spirits of Scotland. Bourbon was my father's whiskey of choice. He was not allergic to corn. Dad sparingly enjoyed "one or two fingers" of bourbon over ice, usually to celebrate the end of a hard day. Pouring that drink for my father was as close as I would get to bourbon because I wanted to continue to enjoy good health.

Although the allergy kept me in the gin-drinking camp for many years, I now believe that bourbon is an amazing spirit. I love the history, the lore, and the beverage. No other spirit has developed as quickly and as successfully as bourbon.

There are specific days that change the course of events in one's professional career—and in my case drinking preferences. From 1999 to 2016 I was based in the head and heart of bourbon country, Louisville, Kentucky, teaching culinary arts at Sullivan University's National Center for Hospitality Studies. During this time I attended the 2002 annual conference of the International Association of Culinary Professionals (IACP) in San Diego and was fortunate to experience a succession of days that were transformational both for my career and for my preferences in spirits.

The conference program at the IACP is always informative, but this year was special for me because I was attending, in part, to accept the inaugural scholarship for graduate study in gastronomy at the University of Adelaide. The university and Le Cordon Bleu International partnered to offer a program that would lead to a master of arts focusing on the culture of food and drink. At the conference Le Cordon Bleu International hosted a special limited seating dinner for alumni, award winners, and other interested IACP members. Each course of the dinner was conceptualized and supervised by one of the many talented chefs from one of the many legendary Le Cordon Bleu campuses worldwide. It goes without saying that the food was outstanding. That night I had the good fortune to be seated at the same table as Katrina Markoff. From Vosges Haut-Chocolat in Chicago, she is a Le Cordon Bleu Paris graduate and IACP award winner. She was honored by the IACP that year for her skills and innovation with chocolate. I enjoyed meeting her and the conversation was one that I will always remember. After meeting an amazing entrepreneur like Markoff and listening to her story of success, I consider every trip to Chicago incomplete without a trip to her shop to sample her latest creation—this despite the fact that Markoff and I have had limited contact since; and I would be surprised if she would even remember me. This is a good lesson about how connecting with a story and a person can influence future purchases.

After the dinner, a friend and fellow IACP attendee invited me to meet for a drink with Lincoln Henderson, then Brown-Forman's master distiller, who was in town to present at the conference. When this bourbon legend offered to buy our group a drink, I thanked him but voiced concern. "Mr. Henderson, thank you, but I am allergic to corn." He replied, "Son, what you are allergic to is distilled out of the drink. Tonight, you're drinking bourbon." I did, the bourbon was delicious, and I experienced no ill effects.

That encounter with a master distiller from the Commonwealth of Kentucky changed the trajectory of my career and my personal preferences. I started drinking more bourbon. I started cooking with bourbon. For the record, I still drink gin and sometimes Scotch, but more often than not bourbon is the spirit in my glass when I drink alcohol. While I enjoy all bourbon, I have found some that I really savor. I keep a small gathering of bourbon bottles for all occasions: bottles for cocktails, bottles for everyday drinking, and a small group of bottles for special events, such as the day in 2003 I was honored by Governor Paul Patton with a commission as a Kentucky Colonel and the day that I graduated with my master of arts in gastronomy from the University of Adelaide. I also celebrate finishing writing a new book with a glass of bourbon.

Another spring, another IACP conference, and another master distiller. In 2008 I attended a dinner at the Dickie Brennan Bourbon House in New Orleans during the conference. This dinner featured a bourbon pairing with each course and was led by Master Distiller Harlen Wheatley from Buffalo Trace. At the end of the meal I walked out on Bourbon Street and wondered how chefs use bourbon in cooking. The same year I met another master distiller at another conference in the Big Easy, this one hosted by the Society of Wine Educators (SWE). During their national conference, they held the inaugural training and exam for their designation certified specialist of spirits (CSS). I attended this training, led by Master Distiller Chris Morris of Brown-Forman and Woodford Reserve, and was thrilled when I passed the certification exam. Yes, you guessed it—time for some celebration bourbon. The same week, I passed the SWE's certified specialist in wine exam and, ironically, I celebrated with another glass of bourbon. The result of this academic inquiry, both wondering how chefs were using bourbon in cooking and the specifics of all spirits, led to *The Kentucky Bourbon Cookbook*, which won the 2010 Gourmand Award for Best Book for Cooking with Drinks in the World.

After the publication of *The Kentucky Bourbon Cookbook,* I was honored when Jim Beam invited me to cook at a meal they hosted during the 2010 Kentucky Bourbon Festival. I was excited to share the stage with Beam's Master Distiller Fred Noe. After the book won the Gourmand Award, Jim Beam invited me to cook again in 2011. I also became a regular panel speaker along with Master Distillers Chris Morris, Parker Beam, Craig

Beam, Fred Noe, Jim Rutledge, and Jimmy Russell. Others on the panels included Julian Van Winkle, Al Young, Mike Veach, Susan Reigler, Joy Perrine, Fred Minnick, Bernie Lubbers, Josh Hafer, Larry Kass, Chuck Cowdery, and Peggy Noe Stevens, to name a few. I am still very honored to have been included on those panels as a bourbon expert. For me, the best part of participating in these panels is the opportunity to meet and learn from some of bourbon's greatest minds. Usually I speak only on the subject of cooking with bourbon. I value the chance to learn as much as I can from the bourbon icons next to me on the panel. The results are the lessons and knowledge in the pages of this book. I will discuss some of the lessons I learned on these panels about bourbon and will include stories of my encounters with some of the greats in the bourbon world.

In your bourbon-learning journey explore as many bourbons as you can—and take notes. Take notes in your mind and in a notebook. Listen more than you talk about bourbon. Listen to the experts, listen to your friends, but most important listen to your reaction to the bourbon in your glass. Know that it is okay for your reaction to differ from those of your friends and the experts. In many ways, you enter your own bubble when you drink bourbon. A bubble where you are interacting with your friends and family but at the same time experiencing something unique, something special, something that no one else on earth gets to experience: your own reaction to and relationship with America's native spirit. The more you listen to your reaction, the easier it will be to identify what you like in bourbon and what you should be seeking in bourbon. Once you find a favorite bourbon, hold onto that information but allow yourself to update that choice as you explore more bourbons. Above all, always remember that bourbon is to be enjoyed, savored. Once you find the bourbons that satisfy your palate in ways that only you appreciate, relax and pour yourself a glass. Drink some bourbon! I hope these ten lessons on bourbon will help you on your path to enjoying the world's greatest spirit. Cheers!

# LESSON 1

# THE BOURBON TASTING KIT AND THE BOURBON LEXICON

**W**ELCOME TO THE AMAZING WORLD OF BOURBON, AND congratulations on your commitment to the study of America's native spirit! You are about to meet some great people and have some wonderful experiences. Drinking bourbon helps to facilitate friendships. People with whom you have nothing else in common may become close friends over a glass of this amber spirit. Bourbon is fun to talk about, and comparing notes is a great way to learn. My hope is that you emerge from this book ready to taste many bourbons and, perhaps, find the perfect one (or eight) for you.

As your guide, I will try to avoid expressing opinions that may sway or influence your judgment. After all, this is your journey, not mine. I will tell stories in these lessons and may name specific brands, but each story has a point to help guide your experience. Ultimately, what will become your favorite bourbon is *your* decision and could be based on many things, including but not limited to flavor, aroma, a personal experience, a connection with the brand, or just a fun time with friends. I have found that the most important factor is my reaction to the bourbon in the glass in front of me. The bourbons that I want to taste are the ones that leave me wanting more—even if the "more" is enjoyed at a later date.

Before you get too deep into your study of bourbon, you will need to purchase a few items. All students need supplies! The following sections offer advice on assembling a *tasting kit,* an essential tool for evaluating bourbon.

The essentials of a tasting kit. *OlgaMiltsova/iStock.com*

# ITEMS FOR YOUR TASTING KIT

## A NOTEBOOK FOR OBSERVATIONS

This notebook does not have to be fancy, but it is important. You can record notes on bourbon to revisit at future dates. You should make notes on the name, the price, the color, the proof, the age, the aroma, and specific attributes you detect. For bottles that come with batch numbers, take note of that too. I have found variations in batches where I prefer one over another of the same brand.

You can score on a scale of 1–5, 1–10, or 1–20, or you can rate the bourbon on a 100-point scale, as is done with some wines. You can give the bourbon stars: no stars if you don't like the whiskey to 5 stars if you are a big fan. The exact system doesn't matter as long as you are consistent. I try to stick to a three-level scale: "exceeds expectations," if I am really impressed; "meets expectations"; and "disappointed." Sometimes this assessment is tied to price. The more I spend, the higher the bar to exceed expectations. Recently I ran across a whiskey at a low price and was pleasantly surprised to find it "exceeded expectations." Was it the best whiskey ever? No, but for the price . . . I would buy it and drink it again. I have also spent money on expensive bourbons that were every bit as good and perhaps better than the inexpensive bourbon but were "disappointing" because of how much they cost. I also try to leave a sentence or two about my experience with the whiskey, explaining how and why it met, fell short of, or exceeded expectations.

# AT LEAST ONE CLASSIC BOURBON

The next item you will need is bourbon! We'll start with classic bourbon, followed by suggestions for "wheated" and "high-rye" varieties. I have listed some well-known, reliable brands in each category. To start, I suggest that you have one bourbon from each list. Try them separately and in a flight against one another so that you can find which bourbon you prefer. Try them in cocktails. When you run out of one bourbon, you can replace it with another from the list and, eventually, branch out and try bourbons that are not in these lists.

**BAKER'S.** Small batch from Jim Beam, aged 7 years and bottled at 107 proof (53.5% ABV).

**BLACK MAPLE HILL.** Small batch from Kentucky Bourbon Distillers. No age statement, but rumors suggest it is a blend averaging 8 years and bottled at 95 proof (47.5% ABV).

**BOOKER'S.** Small batch from Jim Beam. Age varies from batch to batch ("It's ready when it's ready"), and it is bottled uncut from the barrel, putting it somewhere around 125 proof (62.5% ABV).

**BUFFALO TRACE.** From the Buffalo Trace Distillery, bottled at 90 proof (45% ABV).

**EAGLE RARE.** From the Buffalo Trace Distillery, aged a minimum of 10 years, and bottled at 90 proof (45% ABV). Also bottled at 17 years and 20 years ("Double Eagle Very Rare").

**ELIJAH CRAIG.** Small batch from the Heaven Hill Brands, named for the "father of bourbon." No age statement, bottled at 94 proof (47% ABV). Also bottled at barrel proof, with a toasted barrel finish, 18 years old and in a straight rye.

**ELMER T. LEE.** Named for the long-serving master distiller at Buffalo Trace Distillery. No age statement, and bottled at 90 proof (45% ABV).

**EVAN WILLIAMS.** Named for an early distiller of bourbon by Heaven Hill Brands. No age statement, and bottled at 86 proof (43% ABV). Also available in a 100-proof (50% ABV) bottled-in-bond, a 90-proof (45% ABV) small batch, and a single barrel "vintage" at 86.6 proof (43.3% ABV).

**EZRA BROOKS.** A fantastical name brand acquired by Lux Row Distillers. No age statement, and bottled at 90 proof (45% ABV). Also available in 99 proof (49.5% ABV), 7-year-old-barrel strength "Old Ezra" blended whiskey, straight rye, and bourbon cream.

**GEORGE T. STAGG.** Named for a historical distiller by Buffalo Trace Distillery. No age statement, uncut and unfiltered, barrel proof.

**HEAVEN HILL.** Named for the distillery, this bourbon is 7 years old and bottled at 100 proof (50% ABV) bottled-in-bond.

**JIM BEAM.** Named for the man who started the distillery, this bourbon is 4 years old, 80 proof (40% ABV). Also available in a Single Barrel 95 proof (47.5% ABV), Double Oak, Devil's Cut, rye, and Jim Beam Black Extra Aged labels, 86 proof (43% ABV).

**KNOB CREEK.** Small batch by Jim Beam. Named for the creek that ran through President Abraham Lincoln's boyhood homestead, this bourbon is 9 years old, 100 proof (50% ABV). Also available in a 12-year, 100 proof (50% ABV); rye, 100 proof (50% ABV); Single Barrel, 120 proof (60% ABV); Reserve Single Barrel, 120 proof (60% ABV); Single Barrel Select Rye, 115 proof (57.5% ABV); and Smoked Maple, 90 proof (45% ABV).

**NOAH'S MILL.** Small batch by Willett Distillery, no age statement, 114.3 proof (57.15% ABV).

**OLD CHARTER.** Named for the famous Connecticut Charter Oak. Brand produced by the Buffalo Trace Distillery, no age statement, 80 proof (40% ABV).

**OLD CROW.** Named for James C. Crow, the founder of the brand. Now owned and produced by Beam Suntory, no age statement, 86 proof (43% ABV).

**OLD FORESTER.** Reportedly named for Dr. William Forrester (the extra "r" was removed). Now owned by Brown-Forman, this bourbon comes in several versions, including the "classic" variety at 86 proof (43% ABV). Other versions range in proof up to 120 proof (60% ABV). They also have a Mint Julep version at 60 proof.

**OLD TAYLOR.** Named for Edmund Haynes Taylor Jr., an early distiller and the grandnephew of the twelfth president, Zachary Taylor. The brand is owned and produced by the Buffalo Trace Distillery at 80 proof (40% ABV). The premium brand Colonel E. H. Taylor is available in small batch, single barrel, and barrel proof versions.

**PURE KENTUCKY.** Produced by Willett Distillery, this small batch bourbon has no age statement and is offered at 107 proof (53.5% ABV).

**ROWAN'S CREEK.** A small batch bourbon produced by Willett Distillery with no age statement at 100.1 proof (50.05% ABV).

**WATHEN'S.** A single barrel bourbon produced by the Medley Family. No age statement, bottled at 94 proof (47% ABV).

**WILD TURKEY.** The brand is owned by the Campari Group and offers a wide range, including the no age statement 81 proof (40.5% ABV) and 101 proof (50.5% ABV). They also produce aged bourbons and a line of Russell's Reserve, named for the Master Distiller Jimmy Russell.

**WOODFORD RESERVE.** A small batch bourbon produced by Brown-Forman with no age statement at 90.4 proof (45.2% ABV). They also produce a double-oaked Woodford Reserve, a Master's Collection, a Batch Proof, a Distillery series, a commemorative Kentucky Derby Bottle, and their premier Baccarat Edition.

## AT LEAST ONE "WHEATED" BOURBON

As the name implies, wheated bourbons feature a higher ratio of wheat in the recipe, or *mash bill*.

**LARCENY.** Heaven Hill's premium version of the Old Fitzgerald brand, it is considered a small batch variety. No age statement, bottled at 92 proof (46% ABV). Also available in barrel proof.

**MAKER'S 46.** Maker's Mark's premium version of the classic product is finished with seared French oak staves, with no age statement at 94 proof (47% ABV).

**MAKER'S MARK.** A small batch bourbon owned by Beam Suntory. The dripping red wax top and squarish bottle are distinctive. No age statement at 90 proof (45% ABV). Maker's Mark is also available in a 101-proof, Cask Strength, Private Selection with various wood finishes.

**OLD FITZGERALD.** Named for John E. Fitzgerald, the founder of the brand now owned by Heaven Hill Brands.

High wheat bourbon. *Andrei Iakhniuk/Shutterstock.com*

Offered in an 8-year, 100-proof (50% ABV) bottled-in-bond.

**OLD RIP VAN WINKLE.** A 10-year-old bourbon produced by the Buffalo Trace Distillery that is sometimes confused with Pappy Van Winkle. Old Rip Van Winkle is bottled at 107 proof (53.5% ABV). A 12-year expression is also produced as Van Winkle Special Reserve at 90.4 proof (45.2% ABV).

**PAPPY VAN WINKLE.** Produced by Buffalo Trace Distillery, this super-premium brand is available in Family Reserve bottles aged 15 years, 107 proof (53.5% ABV); 20 years, 90.4 proof (45.2% ABV); and 23 years, 95.6 proof (47.8% ABV). This brand also boasts a Van Winkle Family Reserve Rye.

**REBEL YELL.** Produced by Lux Row Distillers with no age statement, this bourbon is bottled at 80 proof (40% ABV) with a very approachable price.

**W. L. WELLER.** Named for William Larue Weller, an early distiller in Kentucky, this bourbon is produced by Buffalo Trace Distillery, offering a range of products from 90 to 107 proof (45%–53.5% ABV). The 12-year expression is bottled at 90 proof.

High rye bourbon. *Smit/Shutterstock.com*

## AT LEAST ONE HIGH-RYE BOURBON

Bourbon enthusiasts will recognize a few familiar brands in this category. High-rye bourbons are common and, thus, essential in a tasting kit.

**ANCIENT AGE.** Buffalo Trace Distillery produces several products with the Ancient Age label: 80 proof (40% ABV), 90 proof (45% ABV), and Ancient Ancient Age 10 star at 90 proof (45% ABV).

**BASIL HAYDEN'S.** A small batch bourbon produced by Beam Suntory at 80 proof (40% ABV), with no age statement.

**BLANTON'S.** Named for Albert B. Blanton, an early leader at the Buffalo Trace Distillery, where this bourbon is produced. The brand launch was led by Master Distiller Elmer T. Lee. Four expressions are available: the original 93 proof (46.5% ABV), 103 proof (51.5% ABV), Blanton's Gold, and Cask Strength Blanton's.

**BRECKENRIDGE.** The brand is named for the city where they distill, Breckenridge, Colorado. The award-winning bourbon from the world's highest distillery was acquired by Tilray, a global cannabis company, in 2021. The bourbon is aged for a minimum of 3 years and is bottled at 86 proof (43% ABV).

**BULLEIT.** Named for the Bulleit Family, which started distilling in 1830, the brand is now owned by Diageo. Bulleit bourbon is bottled at 90 proof (45% ABV). They also produce a 10-year-old bourbon at 91.2 proof (45.6% ABV), a cask strength bourbon that has a range between 118 and 125 proof (59%-62.5% ABV), and a rye.

**FOUR ROSES.** The brand is named for the Rose family: the founder, Rufus Mathewson Rose, his brother Origen, and their two sons. The brand is owned by the Kirin Brewery Company. The Four Roses brand is aged 5 years at 80 proof (40% ABV); Four Roses Small Batch is aged 6 to 7 years and bottled at 90 proof (45% ABV); Four Roses Single Barrel is aged 7 to 9 years and bottled at 100 proof (50% ABV); Four Roses Small Batch Select is aged 6 to 7 years and bottled at 104 proof (52% ABV). They also have a line of limited-edition bottles.

**OLD GRAND-DAD.** A brand of bourbon produced and owned by Beam Suntory. The "Old Grand-Dad" refers to Meredith Basil Hayden Sr., who is the namesake of another Beam brand, Basil Hayden. There are three expressions of Old Grand-Dad: 80 proof (40% ABV), 100 proof bottled-in-bond (50% ABV), and 114 proof (57% ABV).

THE BOURBON TASTING KIT AND THE BOURBON LEXICON   ●   13

Smelling, or *nosing*, bourbon is an important part of the tasting process. *Oskars Kupics/Shutterstock.com*

## TASTING GLASSES

Once you've got your bourbon, you will need a set of *clear* tasting glasses. These can be Glencairn whiskey glasses or small wineglasses, as long as they are clear, free of marks such as engravings or cuts in the glass, and have a rounded shape so that you can rotate the bourbon in the glass. You want to be able to see your bourbon.

Prepare for your first taste test by setting up three tasting glasses with the three whiskeys that you have picked from the lists above. Make sure that you have one classic bourbon, one high-wheat bourbon, and one high-rye bourbon. Pour the glasses yourself. Look at the bourbon. Smell the bourbon. Taste the bourbon. Read the labels on the bourbon bottles. See if you can tell the difference between the three. Keep notes on your experience. You may feel a little silly at first, but the more you do this the better you will become at tasting bourbon. Keep these three bottles of bourbon in stock until at least the third lesson in this book ... be forewarned: there is going to be a test! A taste test! Once you have finished your tasting, make sure that you take a little time to learn as much as you can about each bourbon, the distillery where it was produced, the master distiller who was in charge of producing the bourbon, and what some critics think about the bourbon. Make sure that you take the opinions of others with a grain of salt. Remember that you like what you like in bourbon. Someone else should not influence your likes and dislikes. They can offer an opinion, but yours is just as valid as theirs.

# BOURBON TERMS

As you begin your study of America's native spirit, you will want to become familiar with the language that is used in the industry and by connoisseurs and aficionados. The words and definitions below will help you to evaluate bourbon, discuss bourbon, and interact with bourbon experts. Use these terms in your notebook as you taste bourbons, record your opinions, and document what you like and what you don't. These are snapshots in time of your experience. This tool will become very valuable in the future as you look back at your bourbon journey, because opinions sometimes change with greater experience.

*Aftershots*: see Feints.

*Age statement*: A statement on the label that defines the lower age limit of the youngest whiskey in the bottle. All bourbon aged less than four years must carry an age statement on the label. For older whiskey an age statement many times justifies the price. The age statement is not a quality statement.

*Alcohol by volume (ABV)*: An international standard of measure denoting how much alcohol is in a bottle by percentage. In the United States, bottles often carry a measurement of alcohol in "proof," which is double the ABV. Most bottles of bourbon carry a statement of both ABV and proof.

## THE ANGEL'S SHARE

NEW FILL    4 YEARS    18 YEARS

Tracking the evaporation process: the angel's share increases over time.

**Angel's share**: The amount of whiskey lost to evaporation during the aging process. This loss is subject to temperature, humidity, and the size and location of the barrel in the rickhouse (see below for definition). The loss of whiskey makes what remains more valuable.

**Backset**: In a sour-mash whiskey, the backset is an acidic sample of the primary distillation that is added back to the mash tub to help with the fermentation and to safeguard the fermentation from bacterial contamination.

**Barrel (cask)**: The standard bourbon (whiskey) barrel holds 53 gallons. Bourbon standards require that

FabrikaCr/iStock.com

a new barrel be made from white oak and be charred on the inside. Barrels may not be reused to make bourbon; however, many bourbon barrels are subsequently used to make Scotch, aged rum, and tequila.

**Batching (batch)**: The contents of a group of barrels that are blended together before bottling.

**Bottled by**: A label marking used by distillers and rectifiers (see definition below) to indicate who bottled the bourbon.

**Bottled-in-bond (BIB)**: To carry the label bottled-in-bond a bourbon must be from one distillation season, by one distiller, at one distillery.

Then the bourbon must be aged at a federally bonded warehouse under US government supervision for at least four years and bottled at 100 proof (50% ABV). Many consumers consider this designation to be a quality statement. In the past, that assumption was true, but with the plethora of bourbons available bottled-in-bond, the designation now only speaks to the extra regulations that govern it.

**Bottling proof**: The proof level that a whiskey enters the bottle to be sold. For the most part whiskey is watered down a little coming out of the barrel before it is bottled. The minimum bottling proof for bourbon is 80 proof (40% ABV).

**Bourbon**: An American whiskey made from at least 51% corn that is aged in a new, charred, white oak container. The spirit is distilled to no more than 160

Bottles labeled with barrel number, bottled-in-bond designation, and proof level. *Courtesy of the Kentucky Distillers' Association*

Barrel with bung. *Photo by Charles Folscher*

proof (80% ABV), enters the barrel at no more than 125 proof (62.5% ABV), and is bottled at a minimum of 80 proof (40% ABV). This type of whiskey was first created in the late 1700s.

**Bung**: A wooden or plastic stopper that is pounded into the bunghole to seal a barrel for storage.

**Bunghole**: A hole in a barrel that is capped with a bung or a large cork. The bunghole is used as an opening in the barrel to empty the contents of the barrel (the bourbon) after the aging process is complete.

**Cask strength**: The proof or ABV at which a whiskey is stored in a barrel. Generally, for bourbon in Kentucky, the cask strength ABV increases during storage because of the new barrels and temperature. By law, bourbon may not enter a barrel at more than 125 proof, or 62.5% ABV. Some producers sell a cask strength bourbon, but usually it is diluted to a more palatable proof or ABV. This dilution also makes the whiskey less expensive. Also known as barrel proof or barrel strength.

**Charring (char)**: The practice of charring exposes the inside of the barrel to intense heat so as to burn it until it resembles the remains of an extinguished campfire. The level of char is rated by time. For example, level 1 takes 15 seconds, level 2 takes 30 seconds, level 3 takes 35 seconds, and level 4 takes 55 seconds. There are even higher levels of char, but most distillers use a level 4 char, also referred to as an "alligator char" because the inside of the barrel resembles alligator skin. The char works to reduce the harsh elements of the alcohol while adding flavors like caramel, honey, and vanilla. The charred barrel is responsible for the sweet, smooth, mellow flavor of the bourbon. The char also imparts an amber color into the spirit.

**Clock the barrel (clocking barrels)**: The practice of arranging a barrel in the rickhouse so that the bunghole sits at 12 o'clock, or on the top of the barrel, to help reduce the amount of whiskey that is lost during storage.

The charring process. *Brymer/Shutterstock.com*

A continuous still. *Jake Hukee/Shutterstock.com*

**Congener**: Chemical byproducts of distillation, including tannins, methanol, esters, and acetone, to name a few. Congeners are responsible for the taste and aroma of a distilled alcoholic beverage.

**Continuous still (column still)**: A continuous still is one that works continuously without regard to batches. This type of still is set up with different levels. As the liquid heats up, the vapor travels up the still with the lightest vapors, the ones with the lowest boiling points, traveling to the top and heavier vapors, the ones with the highest boiling points, staying behind to be discarded.

**Cooper**: Someone who makes or repairs wooden casks or barrels.

**Cooperage**: The workshop or business of a cooper.

**Corn**: The primary grain used to make bourbon. By law, every bourbon must be made from a grain mixture of at least 51% corn. There is no upper limit to the amount of corn that can be used to make bourbon, which means that distillers can use 100% corn if they so choose. Most bourbon makers use a higher percentage than 51%.

A cooper, or barrel maker. *izikMD/Shutterstock.com*

**Devil's cut**: A term coined by the Jim Beam Distillery to describe the whiskey "lost" to absorption into the oak barrel container. Jim Beam has developed a process to extract that lost bourbon, which they bottle and market as a product by the same name.

**Distillation**: The process of separating substances from a liquid by using boiling and condensation. In the case of bourbon, the alcohol is extracted from a corn mash or corn beer. Alcohol boils at 173.1 degrees Fahrenheit. As the still

A bottle of Jim Beam Devil's Cut.
*barinart/Shutterstock.com*

A distiller checks the unaged spirit. *SolStock/iStock.com*

heats up, that alcohol-laden vapor rises to the top of the still and down into the condenser. Once in the condenser, the vapor becomes a liquid high in alcohol.

**Distilled by**: A label marking indicating that the bottle of bourbon was distilled by the same distillery selling it.

**Distiller**: A person or a company that creates bourbon or other spirits.

**Distiller's beer**: A fermented alcoholic liquid used by a distiller to produce a distilled spirit. In the case of bourbon, the distiller uses a grain mixture of at least 51% corn to make a distiller's beer. This beer is loaded into the still, where it is distilled into "white dog" (see below) before it is aged into bourbon. Also referred to as "wash" (see below).

**Distillery**: A facility in which bourbon is distilled.

Wild Turkey Bourbon Distillery in Lawrenceburg, Kentucky. *Irina Mos/Shutterstock.com*

**Doubler**: A type of still pot used for the second round of distillation in American distilling. The doubler receives the spirit that has already been condensed into a liquid.

**Dram**: Officially a dram is defined as ⅛ of a fluid ounce but the term is used informally to describe a small amount of whiskey.

**Ethanol**: Drinking alcohol or grain alcohol ($C_2H_5OH$). Ethanol is naturally created by yeast fermenting sugar into alcohol and carbon dioxide. The carbon dioxide usually dissipates, leaving the alcohol behind. Ethanol is the active drug in alcoholic beverages.

**Expression**: A different version of the same whiskey. Some distillers use the same recipe for their whiskey but at the end of the production change the proof or the age, the position in the rickhouse, or all of the above to create a "different whiskey."

**Extraction**: The flavor and aroma compounds that bourbon pulls from the barrel in which it ages. These compounds can vary from barrel to barrel, which is why some bourbon is mingled while other bourbon is sold from a single barrel.

**Fake tan**: A derogatory term used by whiskey drinkers to describe a deeper color in a whiskey that may be created by the producer by adding caramel color to the whiskey. This practice is banned and outside of the laws governing the production of bourbon.

**Feints**: In the distillation process the feints are the final spirits produced from a spirit still. Also known as the aftershots or the tails. The feints are usually discarded or redistilled.

**Fermentation**: The natural process of yeast consuming sugar and producing alcohol and carbon dioxide.

**Finger**: A measurement of whiskey achieved by filling the glass to the top of a finger that is wrapped around the bottom of the glass. Customers can order whiskey by the finger; for example, "Two fingers of bourbon, please."

**Finish**: The final flavors of bourbon (or any whiskey) on the palate after the bourbon is consumed. The flavors will linger and change in the mouth the longer the taster waits.

Angel's Envy bourbon is finished in port wine barrels. *The Image Party/Shutterstock.com*

**Finishing**: A process wherein bourbon makers transfer a finished product from the original aging barrel into a "finishing barrel" for a final or finishing maturation. The finishing barrels are usually used barrels that once held port wine, sherry, or rum. This finish gives a unique flavor profile to the bourbon.

**Flavored bourbon**: A bourbon base with added flavors such as honey, cinnamon, cherry, peach, vanilla, and maple (which is also available in a smoked variety). These products are only technically bourbon because by law nothing can be added to bourbon.

**Flavoring grain**: The additional grain, beyond the legally required 51% corn, in bourbon that usually determines the flavor. Wheat and rye are the two flavoring grains for bourbon. The wheat profile helps to produce a smoother, sweeter bourbon, while rye produces a spicier bourbon.

**Flipper**: A person who marks up and resells bottles of bourbon on the secondary market.

**Foreshot**: In the distillation process the foreshots are the first spirits produced from a spirit still. Also known as the heads. The foreshots are usually discarded or redistilled.

**Handcrafted**: An unregulated term to describe whiskey making. Some say that the word equals or invokes authenticity, while others contend that it is a "throwaway term" that says nothing about the authenticity of bourbon. While there is no federal definition for the word, so far the courts have upheld the use of the word on labels, determining that a "reasonable consumer" would not be misled by the term.

**Heads**: See Foreshots.

**Hearts**: The hearts is the most desirable part, the center or middle of the distillation. The hearts comes after the heads (foreshots) and before the tails (aftershots, or the feints). The hearts is collected and bottled or aged.

**High rye**: A bourbon containing a large percentage of rye (20–35%) in the mash bill (see below).

**High wine**: The name for a spirit that has undergone the final distillation and is ready for the aging process. In the case of bourbon, the term indicates a spirit no more than 160 proof (80% ABV) that is ready to be diluted to no more than 125 proof (62.5% ABV) before entering the barrel.

A spirit safe containing either high wine or low wine. *Courtesy of the Kentucky Distillers' Association*

**Honey barrel**: The best or ideal barrel for bourbon, one that produces an outstanding bourbon.

**Honey hole**: A liquor store that sells prized bourbon bottles at or near retail price.

**Juice**: A slang word used to describe the bourbon in a bottle. Juice is used interchangeably with whiskey and bourbon.

**Kentucky chew**: When a bourbon taster sips the bourbon and swishes the bourbon around the mouth, allowing the bourbon to aerate and reach every part of their mouth before swallowing.

**Kentucky hug**: The warm sensation a person feels in the upper body when drinking bourbon.

**Legs**: The teardrop-shaped impressions left on the side of the glass after one has swirled a bourbon as it returns to the bottom of the glass.

**Low wine**: The name for a weak spirit that needs to undergo additional distillation to produce a finished spirit before aging. Generally, once a low wine is distilled again, it becomes a high wine and is ready for aging.

**Made by**: A label marking that means a bourbon was packaged and is being sold by a rectifier who did not distill the whiskey.

**Mash bill**: A specific mixture of grains used to make whiskey. Each distillery has a proprietary recipe for a specific whiskey's mash bill. Sometimes a distillery will use the same mash bill for multiple whiskeys and will differentiate whiskey in the rickhouse by aging longer or placing the whiskey in a different place. A mash bill is sometimes referred to as a mash. Also known as grain bill, grain recipe, and mash recipe.

**Master blender**: An honorific title granted to a top-level blender who has many years of experience in the whiskey

Typical ingredients of a mash bill. *Courtesy of Heaven Hill Distillery*

industry. Generally, this is a title given to Canadian and European whiskey makers.

**Master distiller**: An honorific title granted to a top-level distiller who has many years of experience in the bourbon industry. The master distiller usually determines what products will be made, how they will be made, and the flavor profile of specific products.

**Master taster**: An honorific title granted to an assistant of the master distiller. The master taster usually oversees production, monitors barrels by tasting them, and selects barrels for batching.

**Mingling**: When distillers mix together multiple barrels of whiskey to create a common flavor profile. This is how the bourbon from a distillery will taste the same year to year.

A freshly made oak barrel. *Kelly vanDellen/Shutterstock.com*

The three copper pot stills at Woodford Reserve distillery. *Courtesy of Woodford Reserve*

**Nose (nosing)**: The aroma from a whiskey or a bourbon. Smelling or sniffing a whiskey is referred to as nosing a whiskey. After swirling a whiskey, a taster should bring the glass to their nose with their mouth partially open, then inhale through the nose and the mouth. This will allow the taster to smell the distinctive characteristics of a whiskey.

**Oak**: The primary source of lumber used to create barrels for aging whiskey. The requirement that bourbon be aged in a new oak container gives several other industries business, including the lumber and cooperage industries.

**Oxidation**: The exposure of a whiskey or bourbon to air (oxygen). This process begins when a bottle is opened and continues even if the bottle is closed again. Oxidation allows flavors and aromas to emerge, making this process absolutely necessary. Over time oxidation can negatively affect the flavor of whiskey.

**Palate**: A generic term that refers to someone's ability to appreciate and discern the aromas, flavors, and textures of an alcoholic beverage.

**Pot still (wash still)**: A large vessel used to distill alcoholic spirits. Pot stills

The label on this bottle of Knob Creek indicates that it is 100 proof. *Photo by Nathan Dumlao*

operate on a batch basis, as opposed to a column still, which operates continuously. They are traditionally made from copper.

**Produced by**: A label marking that is similar to "made by," indicating that the whiskey is bottled and sold by a rectifier or someone who did not distill the whiskey.

**Proof**: An American measurement of the alcoholic content of a distilled spirit that is twice the ABV. For example, a bourbon that is 80 proof is 40% ABV.

**Rectifiers**: People who buy and blend bourbon to create a unique product but don't distill their own product.

**Red line**: The area just under the char in whiskey barrels where the sugars caramelize, creating a red line. The term is also used to describe the actual soak line (see below) in the barrel.

**Rickhouse (rackhouse)**: A facility or warehouse in which barrels are stored during the aging process. The barrels are stored on racks, usually on multiple levels. The material of the rickhouse and the placement of the barrel affect the maturation process.

Inside a rickhouse. *Courtesy of Heaven Hill Distillery*

Bottles of Elijah Craig Small Batch bourbon. *The Image Party/Shutterstock.com*

**Single barrel**: A premium (and sometimes a "super-premium") category of whiskey in which a bottle contains an aged spirit from a solitary (or single) barrel.

**Small batch**: A term with no legal definition that refers to a bourbon created from a limited number of select barrels. How many barrels depends on the distillery producing the small batch and is usually relative to the size of the distillery. In other words, a large distillery may use a large selection

of barrels to create a "small batch" compared to a small distillery that uses a smaller selection of barrels. In most cases, small batch bourbons have outstanding flavor, but this is not guaranteed by the designation.

**Soak line**: The line in the whiskey barrel that shows how far the whiskey soaked into the barrel. The soak line is sometimes referred to as the red line.

**Sour mash**: The process of using a small amount of mash from the previous batch, the backset, to "sour" the current mash. This leftover mash is acidic, hence the designation "sour." This process helps defend against bacterial infections of the mash. Most bourbon whiskey is made with sour mash or backset, but many don't declare this on the label.

**Still**: An apparatus used to distill alcoholic spirit.

**Still strength**: Describes the strength of the whiskey or spirit as it flows off the still. Typically, the percentage of alcohol as the high wine flows off the still is very high. For bourbon, the still strength does not exceed 160 proof, or 80% ABV.

**Straight bourbon**: Bourbon that is aged a minimum of 2 years. If the bourbon is aged less than 4 years, an age statement is required on the label reflecting the youngest bourbon in the bottle.

**Sweet mash**: An unsoured mash or whiskey that is made with a fresh fermentation without using any backset.

**Tails**: See Feints.

Buffalo Trace Straight Bourbon Whiskey. *NewStart/Shutterstock.com*

A tun filled with mash. *Mont592/Shutterstock.com*

**Thumper**: A parasitic kettle that is connected to the primary kettle. The benefit of running a thumper is that it allows for secondary distillation without running the distillate a second time. The thumper gets its name from the noise it makes when it is in use.

**Tun**: A large vessel designed to hold the ingredients of a mash to allow the conversion of starches into sugars for fermentation. A tun is usually made from stainless steel or copper.

**Unicorn**: A highly sought-after bourbon, usually a limited edition that is hard to find. Bourbons referred to as unicorns usually provide a once-in-a-lifetime taste experience.

**Wash (wort)**: The liquid portion of the mash. Most bourbon is made with the entire mash, but a few bourbon makers drain off the liquid to then ferment and distill. These bourbon makers are using just the wash or the wort to produce bourbon.

**Wet cake**: The wet grain that is derived from the residue at the bottom of a fermentation.

**Wheated (wheater)**: A bourbon that has a high ratio of wheat in the 49% of the mash that does not have to be corn. Wheated bourbon has a sweet flavor on the palate compared with high-rye bourbon, which displays a spicy flavor.

**Whiskey thief**: A tool used by distillers to remove a small portion of bourbon from a barrel. This allows distillers to monitor or check on the maturation of whiskey in a barrel.

**White dog**: An unaged whiskey. The clear spirit is clear because it has not been aged in a charred barrel. Also known as new spirit, new make, white whiskey, or white lightning.

**Yeast**: A microorganism that converts sugar into alcohol and carbon dioxide. Different strains of yeast produce different flavors. Many distilleries have proprietary strains of yeast.

A whiskey thief. *SergeBertasiusPhotography/Shutterstock.com*

Now it is time for a quiz. For those of you who have test anxiety, relax! This is an open-book exam, there is no time limit, and there is no reason you can't enjoy a glass of bourbon while you take the quiz. Also, rest assured that there are no "gotcha" questions. These questions are designed to reinforce the lesson, not to nitpick your knowledge of the subject.

# QUIZ #1

**1. Which of the following bourbons is considered a "classic" recipe?**

A. Ancient Age

B. Elijah Craig

C. Maker's Mark

D. Pappy Van Winkle

**2. Which of the following bourbons is considered a "wheated" bourbon?**

A. W. L. Weller

B. Knob Creek

C. Woodford Reserve

D. Bulleit

**3. Which of the following bourbons is considered a "high-rye" bourbon?**

A. Baker's

B. Old Fitzgerald

C. Elmer T. Lee

D. Breckenridge

**4. A bourbon that is hard to find might be referred to as a:**

A. Goat

B. Unicorn

C. Elephant

D. Donkey

**5. A small batch bourbon is defined as:**

A. 5 barrels of bourbon

B. 100 barrels of bourbon

C. 1,000 barrels of bourbon

D. There is no legal definition for small batch

**6. Your tasting kit should include which of the following items?**

A. A notebook

B. Clear glasses

C. A classic bourbon

D. All of the above

7. Bottled-in-bond is bottled at what proof?

A. 80

B. 90

C. 100

D. Cask strength

8. A barrel maker is referred to as a:

A. Bung

B. Congener

C. Cooper

D. Dram

9. An age statement defines what about the bourbon in the bottle?

A. The highest age of the whiskey

B. The lowest age of the whiskey

C. An average age of the whiskey

D. None of the above

10. What is the evaporation of whiskey in the barrel referred to as?

A. Backset

B. Angel's share

C. Devil's cut

D. Feints

11. When tasting bourbon, smelling the bourbon is referred to as:

A. Nosing

B. Feints

C. Expression

D. Flipper

12. A liquor store that sells prize bourbons at or near retail price is referred to as:

A. Honey barrel

B. Honey hole

C. Angel's share

D. Flipper

13. What is the most desirable part of the distillation?

A. The heads

B. The hearts

C. The tails

D. The underbelly

14. The rickhouse is:

A. Also known as a honey hole

B. A warehouse where bourbon is stored

C. Cooperage

D. None of the above

15. The word handcrafted on the label:

A. Means good workmanship

B. Indicates authenticity

C. Is misleading

D. Has no legal meaning

# LESSON 2

# HOW BOURBON IS MADE

BOURBON IS A SPECULATIVE BUSINESS: COMPANIES PRODUCE BOURBON based on how they think it will sell in the future. After the unaged whiskey, or *white dog,* trickles from the still, bourbon makers entomb it in charred oak containers, which are placed in a rickhouse to age. Most bourbon makers hold the spirit in captivity for at least four years, but aging can last anywhere from three months to twenty-five years—and sometimes more. The entire time, these oak containers are subject to Kentucky's weather and change of seasons. The spirit evaporates, reducing the overall yield (it's said to be siphoned off by "angels," who enjoy a little of Kentucky's finest from time to time). A bourbon barrel holds fifty-three gallons, or about 265 750-milliliter bottles, but the angels take between 65 and 115 bottles, leaving the distiller between 150 and 200 bottles. So, to recap: distilleries invest money into grain, barrels, and space to hold their investment, trusting that there will be a market for it—and all the while, the product evaporates!

Compare this to vodka makers, who capture their product coming off the still, bottle it, and sell the product as quickly as possible. This allows them the ability to recoup their expenses swiftly and make a profit. Vodka makers don't lose product to evaporation because the spirit moves from the still to the bottle so quickly. They often have their product on shelves within the same season as the distillation process. There is risk, yes—but nothing like what bourbon distillers face. If the vodka is good, the investment is sound. In fact, some wonderful vodka is made by whiskey distillers (yes, even the bourbon producers), helping to cover the bills while whiskey ages in the rickhouse and awaits its sale date.

White dog being added to a barrel. *Courtesy of Heaven Hill Distillery*

Despite all the risks, bourbon distillers are bullish on bourbon sales. So much so that today there are a million more barrels in Kentucky than there are citizens—and the gap is growing. And this does not include all the bourbon made outside of the state. (Yes, bourbon can be produced outside of Kentucky as long as the spirit is a product of the United States.)

# THE GRAIN

Bourbon is made from at least 51% corn. However, very few bourbons contain *merely* 51% corn—that figure is just a minimum. Most bourbons have a higher corn content, somewhere in the 60% to 75% range. Some are 100% corn. Most bourbon is made from a mixture of grains that also includes rye, wheat, and barley. Corn is a good grain to use for whiskey because the grain is sweet. There are a lot of fermentable sugars in corn. With bourbons that have a high wheat content, the wheat only adds or accentuates the sweetness. My father favored wheated bourbons. I happen to enjoy high-rye bourbons, which have a higher rye content. When tasting bourbon with my father, I discovered that my reaction is strongest with high-rye bourbon (although, to be clear, I enjoy all bourbons). Rye adds spiciness to the beverage, which I find enjoyable. Listen to your reaction when you taste bourbon. When you react in a positive way, that is your body telling you what you should be drinking—or at least your preference in bourbon.

## THE WATER

Water is water, right? Wrong! Not all water is created equal. When my sister Gretchen visited me in Louisville, she commented on the water quality. She asked for some bottled water, but we don't keep it in the house. When I told her to drink the water from the tap, she grimaced like only someone from a large East Coast city would understand. But then she poured a glass of water and enjoyed the whole glass. In fact, she poured another and said, "This water is amazing!"

Testing the pH of water. *wakila/iStock.com*

Water is assigned a place on the pH scale; it can be more acidic or more alkaline. Kentucky is famous for its limestone-filtered water, which has an alkaline quality that is perfect for making high-quality bourbon.

## THE WOOD

White oak is the source of barrels for the bourbon and wine industries. Why oak? Oak ensures the safety of the whiskey or whatever liquid is stored inside. This watertight property is not characteristic of all woods. Also, humans like the taste of oak. These two qualities make oak the best option for storing beverages for future enjoyment.

A barrel maker, or *cooper*, may apply fire to the inside of the barrel to change the flavor of the liquid. In the wine industry, the cooper merely toasts the barrel so that flavor can be transferred to the wine with minimal color change. Bourbon barrels, on the other hand, are burned to the point of charring on the inside. This char will maximize the flavor

Whiskey does not need to be made in Kentucky to meet the definition of *bourbon*. This is an example of a bourbon made in Florida. *Photo by Katherine Conrad*

imparted by the barrel to the whiskey. The char will also add an amber color. New barrels with new char will add more color to the whiskey than used barrels with older char.

## THE BOURBON PRODUCTION PROCESS

Bourbon production begins when corn mash is loaded into a large vessel known as a *tun*. Water and yeast are added. The yeast goes to work doing what yeast does, fermenting sugar into alcohol and carbon dioxide. Bourbon must first become a beer before being distilled into a whiskey. *Distiller's beer* can be made from any grain, but in the case of bourbon it mostly comes from a corn mash.

Early stages of the bourbon production process at Woodford Reserve distillery.
*Arne Beruldsen/Shutterstock.com*

## YEAST

Yeast is a single-celled microorganism that is primarily responsible for converting sugar into alcohol and carbon dioxide in a natural biochemical reaction that happens everywhere in the world. Yeast is so small that humans often don't realize it is present. In fact, yeast is on your kitchen countertop, in the air, on your skin, and in your body— it is entirely impossible to escape.

Yeast varies depending on geography. Yeast in Louisville is different from yeast in Bardstown, which is different from yeast where you live. Many varieties or strains of yeast exist in the same city. Each distillery has a different yeast. Some distilleries work with multiple strains of yeast, one for each whiskey they produce.

Bourbon wort fermenting. *Ben Callahan/Shutterstock.com*

Distillation equipment at Old Glory Distillery on the state line of Kentucky and Tennessee. *Alexandra Adele/Shutterstock.com*

These various yeast strains, while functioning in a similar way on the molecular level, lend different flavors and characteristics to bourbon.

## DISTILLATION

Distillation begins when the distiller's beer is loaded into the still and the still is heated up. This process helps to break alcohol's chemical bond with water. Alcohol begins to boil at 173.1 degrees Fahrenheit, compared with water, which boils at 212 degrees. Thus, with controlled heating, the alcohol will vaporize first and rise to the top of the still. The vapor then moves into a condenser, a section of the still that has a cooler temperature. This cool temperature causes the vapor to condense into drops of alcohol and water, which drip off the still in the form of *low wine*. The low wine has a higher concentration of alcohol, having left some of its water back in the boiler. The low wine is then reloaded into the still where it is redistilled, vaporized again, and condensed again: *high wine* is formed and collected by the distiller.

At this point the high wine is captured and stored in charred oak containers, where it eventually becomes bourbon.

## THE BOURBON AGING PROCESS

My father received a gift from one of his professors upon graduating from Austin Presbyterian Theological Seminary: a bottle of twenty-year-old bourbon. Dad treasured the special gift and made sure to keep it safe as we moved from Texas to Louisiana, then back to Texas and then on to Nebraska. To celebrate the twentieth

Barrels of bourbon aging at Woodford Reserve. *James R. Martin/Shutterstock.com*

Woodford Reserve rickhouse. *Courtesy of Woodford Reserve*

anniversary of his ordination, Dad finally cracked the seal. He said to me, "It is not every day that someone gets to enjoy a glass of forty-year-old bourbon." As his eldest child and the only one of legal drinking age, I was able to enjoy a glass of my father's treasured whiskey. I did not tell him at the time that really he was enjoying a twenty-year-old bourbon that he had waited twenty years to enjoy.

Whiskey only ages while in contact with wood—in other words, only in the barrel. As soon as the bourbon leaves the barrel, it remains that age forever. (If only we could all be that lucky—imagine picking the right age and then remaining that way for eternity.)

Each year, as the Northern Hemisphere tilts closer to the sun, we get summertime! The whiskey in the barrel expands and pushes into the wood. Then, with a return to winter, the whiskey retreats from the wood and brings with it the charred goodness from the barrel. As the whiskey ages year after year with the change of the seasons, it expands and contracts within the barrel.

In the rickhouse the barrels are racked on multiple floors. In the summer, as the bourbon warehouse warms up, the heat rises to the top, giving the barrels located there extra attention; the barrels in the middle and those at the bottom receive less heat. This uneven heat distribution allows for differences between the whiskey in the top barrels, the middle barrels, and the bottom barrels. The higher the barrel, the more intense the bourbon tends to be. Also, the heat helps to dictate evaporation, much to the angels' glee. The barrels located at the bottom of the rickhouse tend to take longer to mature. When you see a bourbon aged fifteen-plus years before release, most likely that barrel spent its entire time on the bottom level.

In recent years supplemental aging has been added to some regimens in aging bourbon. For example, some of Jefferson's bourbon is aged at sea, and Angel's Envy is finished in port wine barrels. In the case of Jefferson's bourbon, branded Jefferson's Ocean, the bourbon barrels are loaded onto ships that visit twenty-five ports on five continents, crossing the equator twice. This extra aging boosts the selling price of regular Jefferson's bourbon by more than double. In the case of Angel's Envy, the additional aging of three to six months happens in ruby port wine barrels. The company also makes bourbon with a tawny port barrel finish, a sherry barrel finish, a rum barrel finish, and a cask strength version that is aged for ten years and then finished in port wine barrels.

Angel's Envy bourbon on the bottling line after being aged in port or sherry barrels.
*Courtesy of the Kentucky Distillers' Association*

## TO BLEND OR NOT TO BLEND

Most bourbon is a blend of many barrels. This blending allows for the all-important consistent flavors from bottle to bottle, year to year. This is why single barrels, or "honey barrels," are significant.

Although there is no legal definition for what constitutes a "small batch" bourbon, this term is used to denote a special class of bourbon. The term suggests that the bottle contains bourbon blended from a smaller number of barrels, as compared to the standard process in which barrels are blended freely.

Single Barrel bourbon is considered premium. As the name implies, each bottle is sourced from a single barrel. The bottles are usually marked with both barrel and bottle numbers. Other production details may appear on the bottle as well.

Single-barrel bourbon is considered premium bourbon, because each bottle is sourced from one barrel. *Courtesy of the Kentucky Distillers' Association*

# THE MASTER DISTILLERS

Master distillers are responsible for a distillery's final product. What is a master distiller? How does someone become a master distiller? In some cases, individuals become master distillers by working their way up in a distillery, learning through sweat equity (or sweat education) and becoming knowledgeable about every aspect of bourbon production. Some attend a university and study chemistry. In other cases, becoming a master distiller is a family legacy: one's father, grandfather, and maybe even great-grandfather were master distillers. To be clear, inheriting the title does not make the road to becoming a master distiller any easier—in fact, such individuals have a family reputation to uphold, so the pressure can be more intense. The following list of master distillers is not comprehensive by any means, but it is a good start for someone who is beginning their bourbon study.

**CARL BEAM—JIM BEAM**. Carl Beam was born in Nelson County the nephew of Jim Beam. He and his brother Earl helped their father, William "Park" Beam, to reopen the Jim Beam Distillery after Prohibition. He became known as the "Dean of Distillers" because he trained many distillers, including his sons Baker Beam and David Beam. He also trained Jim Beam's grandson Booker Noe. He is a member of the 2006 class of the Kentucky Bourbon Hall of Fame.

**EARL BEAM—JIM BEAM AND HEAVEN HILL**. Beam was the assistant master distiller at Jim Beam. His brother Carl was the master distiller. Earl was spirited away (sorry for the pun) in 1946 to become the master distiller at Heaven Hill. He is a member of the 2003 class of the Kentucky Bourbon Hall of Fame.

**PARKER BEAM—HEAVEN HILL**. Parker Beam was the master distiller at Heaven Hill Distilleries. The Parker Heritage Collection is named for him. He is a member of the inaugural 2001 class of the Kentucky Bourbon Hall of Fame. In 2015, Beam was honored by the Kentucky Bourbon Hall of Fame with the Lifetime Achievement Award.

**FREDERICK BOOKER NOE JR.— JIM BEAM**. Jim Beam's grandson, Noe was the master distiller for Jim

Parker Beam and his father, Earl Beam, both master distillers. *Courtesy of Heaven Hill Distillery*

Beam for over forty years. Noe is the namesake of Booker's Bourbon, a barrel proof bourbon from Jim Beam's Small Batch Collection. Noe coined the phrase "small batch." He is a member of the 2001 inaugural class of the Kentucky Hall of Fame.

**THE REVEREND ELIJAH CRAIG**. Craig is credited with being the "father" and inventor of bourbon. He owned over one thousand acres in what was then Bourbon County. The town he named Lebanon was renamed Georgetown after the first president of the United States, George Washington. Craig donated land for the founding of Georgetown College. In 1789, Craig founded a distillery. The

Distiller Brent Elliott (left). *Courtesy of the Kentucky Distillers' Association*

legend goes that when one of Craig's barns caught on fire, some barrels were partially burned. He used the barrels anyway to ship the whiskey down the river to New Orleans, a trip that took six months. Customers in New Orleans raved about the "red liquor from Bourbon County." Craig realized he had stumbled upon something special and started reusing fish barrels from New Orleans, which he filled with hay, burned on the inside, and then filled with whiskey. At the time of publication of this book, Craig is not a member of the Kentucky Bourbon Hall of Fame.

**BRENT ELLIOTT—FOUR ROSES.** Elliott is the master distiller at the Four Roses Distillery. He was named master distiller after the long-serving Master Distiller Jim Rutledge retired in 2015. Elliott joined Four Roses in 2005. He was named the Master Distiller/Blender of the Year at the 2020 Icons of Whisky America award ceremony. A native of Owensboro, Kentucky, Elliott graduated from the University of Kentucky with a degree in chemistry.

**EDWIN S. FOOTE—STITZEL-WELLER.** Foote is a hero to all who love wheated bourbon. He started at the Henry McKenna Distillery and quickly showed skill for distilling. He is the distiller responsible for the "juice" that would eventually become Pappy Van Winkle. In 2008, Foote was inducted into the Kentucky Bourbon Hall of Fame.

**ALBERT G. GEISER**. Geiser was the first master distiller at the Buffalo Trace Distillery after Prohibition. He is a member of the Kentucky Bourbon Hall of Fame, class of 2004.

**LINCOLN WESLEY HENDERSON— WOODFORD RESERVE, ANGEL'S ENVY**. Henderson earned a bachelor of science degree in chemistry from the University of Louisville and a master of business administration from Webster University. During his forty years with Brown-Forman, he became the master distiller. Henderson is responsible for creating Woodford Reserve and Jack Daniel's Single Barrel. He retired from Brown-Forman and consulted for a few years before founding Angel's Envy with his son and grandsons, who still run the business. He is a member of the inaugural 2001 class of the Kentucky Hall of Fame.

**DREW KULSVEEN—WILLETT**. Kulsveen is the son of Willett master distiller Even Kulsveen and the grandson of Thompson Willett. The younger Kulsveen has been nominated multiple times for a James Beard Award.

**ELMER T. LEE**. Lee was the master distiller at Buffalo Trace Distillery. He is a native of Franklin County, Kentucky. He served in the Pacific in World War II, then graduated from the University of Kentucky with a bachelor of science in engineering. He started working at the George T. Stagg Distillery, now Buffalo Trace, when Colonel Albert Blanton was the master distiller. Lee, who rose to the rank of master distiller in 1981, was credited as the "father of single barrel bourbon" when he released Blanton's Single Barrel to the market. He officially retired in 1985, but Buffalo Trace named him master distiller emeritus—and he never really retired. A few years after his retirement, Buffalo Trace honored Lee with a single barrel release, Elmer T. Lee Single Barrel. Lee is a member of the 2001 inaugural class of the Kentucky Bourbon Hall of Fame.

**CHARLES W. MEDLEY**. Medley is the seventh-generation master distiller for Wathen's Kentucky Bourbon. He is a member of the 2019 class of the Kentucky Bourbon Hall of Fame.

**CHRIS MORRIS—WOODFORD RESERVE**. A native of Louisville, Kentucky, Morris is a graduate of Bellarmine University. He served as the apprentice master distiller to Lincoln Henderson before being promoted to master distiller of Woodford Reserve and the master distiller for all of Brown-Forman in 2003. He developed the

Master Distiller Jimmy Russell (right) with his son, Master Distiller Eddie Russell.
*Courtesy of the Kentucky Distillers' Association*

Bourbon Flavor Wheel, Tasting Notes for bourbon, and wrote the curriculum for the Society of Wine Educators' certified specialist of spirits. Morris was inducted into the Kentucky Bourbon Hall of Fame in 2017.

**STEVE NALLY—MAKER'S MARK AND BARDSTOWN BOURBON COMPANY**. Nally was the master distiller at Maker's Mark for more than thirty-three years before joining the Bardstown Bourbon Company as the master distiller. He is a member of the 2007 class of the Kentucky Bourbon Hall of Fame.

**FRED NOE III—JIM BEAM**. Noe is a graduate of Bellarmine University. He is the great-grandson of Jim Beam and the son of Booker Noe. He became the master distiller for Jim Beam in 2007. Noe is also the ambassador of the Small Batch Collection of bourbons made at the Jim Beam Distillery. He is a member of the 2013 class of the Kentucky Bourbon Hall of Fame.

**DAVID PICKERELL—MAKER'S MARK AND OTHER DISTILLERIES**. Known as the Johnny Appleseed of American whiskey, Pickerell was the master distiller at Maker's Mark for fourteen years, during a time when the brand expanded sales from under 175,000 cases to close to a million cases a year. Later Pickerell founded Oak View Spirits, a consulting company, where he helped to develop over one hundred small distilleries in the United States, including George Washington's Distillery where he served as the founding master distiller, Whistle Pig, and Blackened American Whiskey. He graduated from the United States Military Academy with a bachelor of science in chemistry and earned a master's degree in chemical engineering from the University of Louisville.

## JIMMY RUSSELL—WILD TURKEY.

Russell started sweeping floors in a bourbon distillery and over the years rose to become the master distiller at Wild Turkey. He is known in the industry as the Buddha of Bourbon and the Master Distiller's Master Distiller. He is a member of the inaugural 2001 class of the Kentucky Bourbon Hall of Fame. Russell is also a member of the class of 2016 for Lifetime Achievement.

## JIM RUTLEDGE—FOUR ROSES.

Rutledge worked for Four Roses for almost fifty years, twenty as master distiller, before retiring in 2015. But he did not stay retired for long, opening the J. W. Rutledge Distillery, which produces both bourbon and rye brands. He is a

member of the inaugural 2001 class of the Kentucky Bourbon Hall of Fame.

## BILL SAMUELS JR.—MAKER'S MARK.

He is a member of the inaugural class of the Kentucky Bourbon Hall of Fame, 2001. Samuels helped to market Maker's Mark in a way that expanded the brand's influence and visibility worldwide. In 2017 he was honored by the Kentucky Bourbon Hall of Fame with the Lifetime Achievement Award.

## HARLEN WHEATLEY—BUFFALO TRACE.

A native of northern Kentucky, Wheatley earned a bachelor of science in chemistry and a master's degree in chemical engineering before joining the distilling world. He joined what is now the Buffalo Trace Distillery in 1995 and was quickly promoted up the ranks, becoming the master distiller in 2005. Buffalo Trace named their Wheatley Vodka for him. He has been nominated for a James Beard Award multiple times in the Outstanding Wine and Spirits category.

## EVAN WILLIAMS.

Williams was an early distiller in Kentucky in the decade before Kentucky became the fifteenth state (or, in Kentucky's case, "Commonwealth") admitted to the Union. Williams was also the harbor master in Louisville at the Falls of the Ohio River. He is a member of the 2008 class of the Kentucky Bourbon Hall of Fame.

Assistant Master Distiller Elizabeth McCall.
*Courtesy of Woodford Reserve*

For some readers this list will seem far too short, and it does not account for the diversity found in other professions and even in the distilling industry. Yet the landscape of master distillers is changing quickly. Woodford Reserve, for example, recently named a woman, Elizabeth McCall, assistant master distiller. Other distilleries are promoting people who will change the demographics of the bourbon world.

# QUIZ #2

**1. Bourbon barrels must be made from:**

A. White Oak

B. Cedar

C. Cherry

D. Mesquite

**2. A barrel maker is known as a:**

A. Cooper

B. Distiller

C. Bung

D. None of the above

**3. Alcohol boils at what temperature?**

A. 212 degrees Fahrenheit

B. 200 degrees Fahrenheit

C. 190 degrees Fahrenheit

D. 173 degrees Fahrenheit

**4. Which Jim Beam master distiller is immortalized with a cask strength bourbon?**

A. Fred Noe III

B. Booker Noe

C. Harlen Wheatley

D. Chris Morris

**5. Which master distiller helped to found the Woodford Reserve brand and launch Jack Daniel's Single Barrel?**

A. Harlen Wheatley

B. Chris Morris

C. Lincoln Henderson

D. Evan Williams

**6. Which master distiller is known as the "Buddha of Bourbon"?**

A. Chris Morris

B. Booker Noe

C. Jimmy Russell

D. Harlen Wheatley

**7. Which master distiller has a vodka named for him?**

A. Chris Morris

B. Booker Noe

C. Jimmy Russel

D. Harlen Wheatley

**8. Which former Four Roses master distiller later opened his own distillery?**

A. Jim Rutledge

B. Brent Elliott

C. Drew Kulsveen

D. David Pickerell

**9. Which master distiller is known as the Johnny Appleseed of American whiskey?**

A. Edwin Foote

B. Elmer T. Lee

C. David Pickerell

D. Brent Elliott

**10. Which master distiller is known for his wheated bourbons?**

A. Elmer T. Lee

B. Chris Morris

C. Drew Kulsveen

D. Edwin Foote

**11. Which master distiller is known as the "father of single barrel bourbon"?**

A. Elmer T. Lee

B. Chris Morris

C. Edwin Foote

D. Jimmy Russell

**12. Who is considered the "father" of bourbon?**

A. Jimmy Russell

B. Evan Williams

C. The Reverend Elijah Craig

D. Edwin Foote

**13. Which Jim Beam master distiller also serves as the ambassador of the small batch line of products from that distillery?**

A. Booker Noe

B. Fred Noe III

C. Brent Elliott

D. Elmer T. Lee

**14. Which Willett master distiller has been nominated for a James Beard Award?**

A. Harlen Wheatley

B. David Pickerell

C. Steve Nally

D. Drew Kulsveen

**15. Which master distiller spent time at Maker's Mark and Bardstown Bourbon Company?**

A. Drew Kulsveen

B. Steve Nally

C. David Pickerell

D. Brent Elliot

# LESSON 3

# BOURBON HISTORY, REGULATIONS, AND RULES

THE ORIGIN OF THE NAME *BOURBON* IS THE subject of wonderful, legendary suppositions. Perhaps Americans named the whiskey after the royal family of France, the Bourbon Dynasty, to honor them for their support during the American Revolution. There seems to be a lot of other evidence that points to this homage. After all, many towns and cities in Kentucky are named for French cities or people: for example, Paris, Louisville (named for King Louis XVI), and Versailles. Perhaps the liquor was named for the county in Kentucky where the spirit was first distilled, Bourbon County. Or maybe bourbon is named for the street in New Orleans where the whiskey was sold.

My first exposure to bourbon occurred when I was in elementary school in New Orleans. My school, McDonogh 15, was located in the French Quarter on St. Phillip Street between Royal Street and Bourbon Street. At the time I did not associate bourbon, the beverage, with Kentucky; in fact, I am sure I thought that bourbon originated in New Orleans and was so important to the city that they even named a street after it. I did not connect the spirit with the French Royal House of Bourbon, nor had I even heard of a county in Kentucky by the same name. I was acutely aware that alcohol was sold on Bourbon Street because every so often the famous (or perhaps infamous) street's patrons would end up draped over the play equipment of my elementary school, having failed to stumble back to their hotels the night before. Yes, it was always a tourist. But Bourbon Street was not how I was introduced to bourbon: my

Bourbon Street in New Orleans in the early morning. *Sean Pavone/Shutterstock.com*

father, the Reverend Dr. Thomas H. Schmid, exposed me to the beverage. Bourbon was his favorite whiskey.

Dad was the kind of father who allowed me to experience the world and to make decisions and form opinions based on my experience (or inexperience). He did not always agree with my decisions, but he supported me nonetheless in my actions—as long as I could articulate the reasoning behind my decision and was willing to accept the consequences. For example, Dad was once shucking oysters on our back porch in New Orleans East while my parents were entertaining guests with drinks and hors d'oeuvres. He seemed to enjoy the oysters, so I asked for one. My father expressed his doubts: "I'm not sure that you will like oysters, but if you want one I will open one for you." I remember the adults laughing. My father cleanly and skillfully opened the oyster and handed me the half-shell that contained it. He signaled to me to wait so that he could show me how it was done. When he was ready, he tilted back his head and allowed the oyster to slide into his mouth. He looked at me with a smile, swallowed his oyster, and said, "Now, if that oyster goes into your mouth you can't spit it out, you have to finish it."

My reaction was similar to what Anthony Bourdain describes in *Kitchen Confidential*: "I . . . stood up smartly, grinning with defiance." To me it was a personal challenge—of course I am going to finish the oyster! Are you kidding? Although Chef Bourdain was a bit older when he consumed his first oyster, his account was similar to mine—with one exception. He writes, "It tasted of seawater . . . of brine and flesh . . . and somehow . . . of the future." For me it was more like, yes, seawater, I got that; brine, yes, yes; flesh, yes; and somehow . . . mucus! Of all things, mucus! I tried to smile but my eyes started to water and my throat closed instinctively. "What the holy hell! What have I gotten myself into?" I thought, panicking. Finally, after remembering my promise

Pictured here is a variety of types of whiskey, not all of which are bourbon. *monticello/Shutterstock.com*

not to spit out the poor creature, and with all the laughing adults looking on, I forced myself to swallow. Like Bourdain I was able to not only finish my first oyster (and for the record it stayed down) but also realize that I had survived and that the experience was not so bad. The adults stopped laughing and started to congratulate me with pats on the head and back. I just needed a little more age to fully appreciate this particular culinary delight. Fast-forward fifty years, and anytime I'm in New Orleans I feel that it is obligatory to order at least a dozen oysters. The oysters from the gulf are big, juicy, and full of flavor. They are different from oysters sourced from anywhere else in the world. I love them!

One night, after a particularly hard day, my father sat in his chair holding a glass filled with "two fingers" of a dark amber liquid. He slowly sipped his beverage. I asked if I could taste it, but he answered with a definitive, "No, this is an adult drink. But you can smell it if you want." The tone of his voice let me know that this decision was not up for debate. The best I could hope for was to experience the aromas of the whiskey. When I asked him what it was, he said, "Bourbon." I took in a big lungful and was overwhelmed by the aroma of what I would later understand to be alcohol. Many years later, my father and I would discuss the flavors and aromas of bourbon, which we discerned as caramel, vanilla, sweet oak, and licorice. By that time, I was living and working in Louisville, Kentucky, in many ways the center of the bourbon world (although Bardstown is considered the capital of bourbon).

# WHISKEY OR WHISKY?

The journey to become a bourbon connoisseur begins with knowledge and ends in discernment and appreciation for the aged liquor. Bourbon is an American whiskey, but not all American whiskey is bourbon. The word *whiskey* comes from Gaelic *uisge beatha,* which means "water of life." Eventually the Gaelic became *whiskey* in Ireland and *whisky* in Scotland. Bourbon's tradition pulls knowledge from both the Irish and Scottish traditions so there is no uniform spelling for whisk(e)y in the United States. There are examples of both spellings inside the world of bourbon; for example, Maker's Mark is a whisky, while Woodford Reserve is a whiskey. Both are bourbon. (A few other American distillers, such as Old Forester and George Dickel, also spell whisky without the "e.")

Maker's Mark uses the spelling "whisky" for its product, while Woodford Reserve uses "whiskey." *darksoul72/Shutterstock.com* and *The Image Party/Shutterstock.com*

I would find later, while studying at the University of Adelaide, that proper spelling is subjective depending on your country of origin. Ask someone from the British Commonwealth to spell *color* or *flavor,* for instance. Beyond the academic setting, exact spelling does not matter as long as you spell within the norms of the system in which you grew up. In the United States we enjoy both traditions, and thus there are two spellings for the same word. However, it should be noted that the Code of Federal Regulations, Title 27, which defines "the standards of identity" for spirits, uses the spelling "whisky" exclusively, even though most American distilleries use "whiskey."

The alcohol by volume (ABV) of this bottle of Old Forester is 43%, as listed on the label.
*barinart/Shutterstock.com*

## UNDERSTANDING PROOF

New bourbon lovers might look at a bottle of bourbon wondering about the potency of the liquid they are about to consume. When it comes to potency, not all bourbon is the same! You will find this information on the label in two different forms: alcohol by volume and proof. Alcohol by volume (ABV) is the percentage of alcohol present in the bottle. Proof is the ABV doubled. The term *proof* dates to several hundred years ago and comes from England, where alcohol was tested with the "burn or no burn" test. If the alcohol, mixed with gunpowder, ignited when it was exposed to flame, the alcohol was said to be over-proof. If the alcohol did not ignite, it was said to be under-proof. At the time this was a good test to ensure one was purchasing a quality product. The median of this proof was and is 100 proof. This is why alcohol ventures over the 100 proof mark and in fact reaches a theoretical 200 proof. This over-proof/under-proof system was set up to determine the amount of tax the distiller owed the government.

# WHISKEY IN US HISTORY

The Revolutionary War was fought, in part, because the British taxed the American colonists even though they had no representation in the British Parliament. Of course, once the break from Britain was official, the newly formed US Congress, at the suggestion of the first secretary of the treasury, the now-notorious Alexander Hamilton, enacted taxes on alcohol production. This negatively and disproportionately affected farmers because, more often than not, they distilled their crops into spirit, which was easier to transport than corn and wouldn't spoil on its way to market. This tax led to an insurrection of about fifteen hundred farmers now known as the Whiskey Rebellion. President George Washington called up about fifteen thousand militia, and the force invaded Pennsylvania. This was the first time a sitting president personally led troops into battle.

A statue of Alexander Hamilton, who won infamy for enacting taxes on alcohol production—among other deeds. *Bill Perry/Shutterstock.com*

The only other example was when President James Madison commanded troops during the British invasion of Washington, D.C., during the War of 1812 (which lasted from June 18, 1812 to February 17, 1815). First Lady Dolly Madison heroically ran back into the burning Executive Mansion to save the portrait of President Washington. The fact that the British burned the people's house during that invasion led to the building being whitewashed during its reconstruction—thus its new name, the White House.

When I was a student in New Orleans, one of the field trips we took was to the site of the battle of New Orleans in the War of 1812. The hero of that battle was General Andrew Jackson, who would eventually become the seventh president of the United States. In 1815, Kentucky sent twenty-three hundred militiamen to aid the eventual commander in chief at the battle. Jackson, who hailed from Kentucky's southern neighbor Tennessee, acknowledged Kentucky's affinity for whiskey, saying, "I have never in my life seen a Kentuckian who didn't have a gun, a pack of cards, and a jug of whiskey." The battle of New Orleans was brief and incurred fewer than one hundred American casualties. The British did not fare as well, suffering over two thousand

The Whiskey Rebellion in western Pennsylvania, 1794. In this illustration, rebels escort a tarred and feathered tax collector from his burning home. *Everett Collection/Shutterstock.com*

This 1846 illustration by Nathaniel Currier offers a less-than-subtle depiction of the life of an alcoholic, from the first drink to a tragic end. This type of graphic was commonly used to promote the temperance movement. *Keith Lance/iStock.com*

casualties: the commanding officer, Major General Sir Edward Pakenham, and the executive officer, Major General Samuel Gibbs, both died in the conflict, and Major General John Keane was wounded in action.

Very few shots were fired during the Whiskey Rebellion; the United States survived a threat from inside its own borders and from its own citizens. The tax became a permanent enforceable law. Bourbon is taxed by the US government to this day to the tune of about $4 billion.

Later, alcohol production would come under threat again, this time in the form of a constitutional amendment. The seeds for this change to the Constitution were planted in the 1830s when temperance societies started to advocate moderate consumption or complete abstinence from liquor. Some states started to write Prohibition laws in the mid-1850s; however, during the Civil War the country did not have time to try to regulate citizen morality. In 1862, advisors to the sixteenth president, Abraham Lincoln (a Kentucky native), told the president that General Ulysses S. Grant was excessively drinking whiskey. The president replied, "Tell me what brand of whiskey that Grant drinks. I would like to send a barrel of it to my other Generals." Lincoln understood that to win the war the North needed to win battles—a feat Grant accomplished over and over again. After the war, in 1869, Grant would transition from commanding general of the US Army to eighteenth president of the United States, but the issues surrounding alcohol did not go away.

The twenty-seventh president of the United States, William Howard Taft, defined whiskey in the 1909 "Taft Decision" and established regulations surrounding its production. His decision stands today, with a few additions: in 1938 the new barrel requirement was introduced for bourbon, and in 1964 bourbon was defined as a US product exclusively. Later, after his presidency, Taft would preside over the US Supreme Court as the tenth chief justice (1921–1930)—during Prohibition. On the one hundredth anniversary of his decision, William Howard Taft, the only person to serve in the top positions of both the executive branch and the judicial branch of the US government, was inducted into the Kentucky Bourbon Hall of Fame with the class of 2009.

The Eighteenth Amendment to the Constitution was proposed in Congress just before Christmas, December 18, in 1917. A little more than a year later, on January 16, 1919, the amendment was ratified by the requisite number of "legislatures of the several States." This amendment carried several firsts: the first time that an amendment to the

Prohibition agents with a still used to distill hard liquor, November 11, 1922.
*Everett Collection/Shutterstock.com*

Constitution restricted citizens' freedoms; the first time an amendment was proposed
with a time clock (in section 3 of the Eighteenth Amendment, Congress gave the state
legislatures seven years to ratify the proposal or the process would start all over); and
the first time that a constitutional amendment was repealed (in 1933). After passage,
the Eighteenth Amendment prohibited the manufacture, sale, and transportation of
intoxicating liquors, including both importation and exportation. This included all
states and territories subject to the jurisdiction of the United States.

> **Section 1:** After one year from the ratification of this article the manufacture,
> sale or transportation of intoxicating liquors within, the importation thereof

into, or the exportation thereof from the United States and all the territory subject to the jurisdiction thereof for beverage purposes is hereby prohibited.

**Section 2:** The Congress and the several States shall have concurrent power to enforce this article by appropriate legislation.

**Section 3:** This article shall be inoperative unless it shall have been ratified as an amendment to the Constitution by the legislatures of the several States, as provided in the Constitution, within seven years from the date of the submission hereof to the States by the Congress.

Prohibition agents with bottles of wine and liquor confiscated during a raid, October 14, 1922.
*Everett Collection/Shutterstock.com*

Los Angeles customers buying and drinking liquor the day after the Twenty-First Amendment was ratified by President Franklin D. Roosevelt, December 6, 1933. *Everett Collection/Shutterstock.com*

Thus began the US era known as Prohibition, the period of time between the Eighteenth and Twenty-First Amendments. After passage of the Eighteenth Amendment, organized crime in the United States expanded to unprecedented levels. Al Capone and the Purple Gang became famous during this period of time. Speakeasies, or illegal bars, and bootlegging, or the importation and transportation of alcohol, became cash cows for many in organized crime.

The Twenty-First Amendment was proposed on February 20, 1933:

> **Section 1:** The eighteenth article of amendment to the Constitution of the United States is hereby repealed.

*Section 2:* The transportation or importation into any State, Territory, or possession of the United States for delivery or use therein of intoxicating liquors, in violation of the laws thereof, is hereby prohibited.

*Section 3:* This article shall be inoperative unless it shall have been ratified as an amendment to the Constitution by conventions in the several States, as provided in the Constitution, within seven years from the date of the submission hereof to the States by the Congress.

The amendment was ratified by December 5, 1933. The thirty-second president of the United States, Franklin D. Roosevelt, had successfully kept his campaign promise to end Prohibition. Roosevelt's successor, the thirty-third president of the United States, Harry S. Truman, a Missouri native with roots deep in Kentucky, started his day at 5:00 a.m. with an egg, a slice of toast, a slice of bacon, a glass of skim milk, and a shot of Old Grand-Dad, a bourbon now produced by Beam Suntory Brands.

# THE CURRENT DEFINITION OF BOURBON

Here is a short list of guidelines that every bourbon lover should know. Bourbon must meet the following criteria.

**PRODUCED IN THE UNITED STATES, ITS TERRITORIES, OR THE DISTRICT OF COLUMBIA.** Many people believe that bourbon has to be produced in Kentucky, but there are many examples of bourbon produced outside the Commonwealth. Texas, Pennsylvania, North Carolina, and Tennessee are some of the states that have active distilleries producing bourbon. Technically, bourbon could be made in American Samoa, the southernmost territory of the United States; Saint Croix in the United States Virgin Islands, the easternmost territory; or Guam, the westernmost territory.

**MADE FROM A GRAIN MIXTURE THAT IS AT LEAST 51% CORN.** Most bourbons well exceed the 51% corn rule in the mash bill. They are closer to 60% or 70% corn. One of the most important parts of the grain mixture is the part that is not corn. Distillers most

The mash bill for any bourbon must include at least 51% corn. *Aleksandr Porvatkin/Shutterstock.com*

commonly use rye or wheat. Bourbon experts will speak of a "wheated bourbon" or a "high-rye bourbon," both terms referring to the other ingredient in the completed mixture. Bourbon with a corn and wheat mixture tends to be sweet on the palate, while bourbon made with a corn and rye mixture tends to have a spicy finish. Most bourbon connoisseurs know enough to seek out bourbon with a palate that they enjoy.

**AGED IN A NEW, CHARRED OAK CONTAINER.** Please note that the age is not specified, and neither is the shape of the container. Once I was on a panel with the late Parker Beam, the former master distiller for Heaven Hill

The inside of an oak barrel after the charring process. *Razoomanet/Shutterstock.com*

To be labeled "straight bourbon," like the bottle of Knob Creek shown here, a bourbon must be aged for at least two years. *Thomas Trompeter/Shutterstock.com*

Distilleries. He observed to the audience that technically a whiskey could be called bourbon if, as the new spirit sprang from the still, it was captured in a new oak pitcher that was charred on the inside and cut with a little water. Once poured, which could happen at any time, the liquid going into the awaiting glass is bourbon.

**BOURBON HAS NO AGE REQUIREMENT.** However, to be labeled "straight bourbon," it must be aged a minimum of two years. Any bourbon aged less than four years must include an age statement on the label. Bottled-in-bond must be aged for a minimum of four years. If there is an age statement on the label, the age must refer to the youngest whiskey in the bottle.

**DISTILLED TO NO MORE THAN 160 PROOF (80% ABV).** The higher a spirit is distilled, the more its distinctive characteristics disappear. Capping the proof allows some of the corn flavor to remain in the resulting bourbon.

A cask strength or "barrel proof" bourbon (such as Elijah Craig Small Batch, shown here) is sold at a proof approximating its strength when it was first placed in the barrel— typically around 125 proof. *barinart/ Shutterstock.com*

**ENTERED INTO THE CONTAINER AT NO MORE THAN 125 PROOF (62.5% ABV).** As the still produces a spirit that does not exceed 160 proof, the master distiller cuts the spirit with water to reduce the proof to no more than 125.

**NO ADDITIVES OF ANY KIND CAN BE USED TO COLOR OR FLAVOR BOURBON.** Other whiskey makers can add caramel coloring to their whiskey if they are not happy with the color after maturation

and they can tweak the flavor. Bourbon is all natural!

**BOTTLED AT A MINIMUM OF 80 PROOF (40% ABV).** Whiskey is traditionally bottled above 40% ABV. Many Scotch drinkers prefer 43% ABV (86 proof) as the ideal distilling level for that spirit. Bourbon ranges from 80 proof to in excess of 125 proof (62.5% ABV). Bottled-in-bond is always bottled at 100 proof (50% ABV). Cask strength bourbon is at or a little above 125 proof.

If you know these rules you are well on your way to becoming a bourbon connoisseur.

Bourbons labeled as "bottled-in-bond" (such as Evan Williams, shown here) are always bottled at 100 proof. *barinart/ Shutterstock.com*

Because no additives can be used to color or flavor bourbon, these bottles of flavored Jim Beam are labeled as "Liqueur Infused with Kentucky Straight Bourbon Whiskey." *Jonathan Weiss/Shutterstock.com*

# QUIZ #3

**1. Bourbon must be made in:**

A. Kentucky

B. The United States

C. Bourbon County, Kentucky

D. Anywhere in the world

**2. What city is known as the capital of bourbon?**

A. Louisville, Kentucky

B. New Orleans, Louisiana

C. Bardstown, Kentucky

D. Frankfort, Kentucky

**3. The Eighteenth Amendment to the US Constitution limited all of the following except:**

A. Production

B. Transportation

C. Selling

D. Consumption

4. The "proof" of a whiskey is the alcohol by volume:

A. Doubled

B. Tripled

C. Quadrupled

D. None of the above

5. Before the Whiskey Rebellion, who suggested a tax on whiskey to Congress?

A. George Washington

B. Alexander Hamilton

C. Thomas Jefferson

D. James Madison

6. Who said, "I have never in my life seen a Kentuckian who didn't have a gun, a pack of cards, and a jug of whiskey"?

A. George Washington

B. Alexander Hamilton

C. Andrew Jackson

D. James Madison

7. During Prohibition organized crime made money with which of the following:

A. Speakeasies

B. Bootlegging

C. Both of the above

D. None of the above

8. Which president drank a shot of bourbon every morning with breakfast?

A. Franklin D. Roosevelt

B. Andrew Jackson

C. Harry S. Truman

D. George Washington

9. Which of the following amendments to the Constitution of the United States is the only one to repeal another amendment?

A. Eighteenth

B. Nineteenth

C. Twentieth

D. Twenty-First

10. According to law, what makes up most of the mash for bourbon?

A. Corn

B. Wheat

C. Rye

D. Barley

11. Bourbon must be bottled at what proof minimum?

A. 80

B. 90

C. 100

D. 120

**12. Bourbon must be aged in which of the following?**

A. Oak container

B. Cherry wood barrel

C. Stainless steel

D. Concrete

**13. Bottled-in-bond must always be bottled at what proof?**

A. 80

B. 90

C. 100

D. 120

**14. To be labeled "straight bourbon," the whiskey in the bottle must be aged at least:**

A. Two years

B. Four years

C. Five years

D. Six years

**15. Bourbon must not be distilled to more than what proof?**

A. 125

B. 140

C. 150

D. 160

# LESSON 4

# HOW TO TASTE BOURBON

T HE BEST ADVICE I EVER RECEIVED REGARDING TASTING bourbon was from Master Distiller Parker Beam when we served on a tasting panel during the annual meeting of the International Association of Culinary Professionals in Denver in 2009. Parker's wisdom is self-evident but is best revealed once you have formally tasted bourbon. So first, let's dig into tasting bourbon. I want you to pour a glass of bourbon and follow these steps to maximize your enjoyment of our liquid treasure.

A note on picking the proper glass to taste whiskey. The glass should be clear without any writing or engraving on the side. It should be rounded on the sides, like a small wineglass, so that you can easily swirl the whiskey around. You may want to add a little water to the whiskey before you taste. This may help to reveal or "open up" the aromas and flavors of the bourbon.

If you are still having trouble detecting aromas, pour a small amount of bourbon into one hand and then rub your hands together. Hold your hand in front of your nose and mouth and breathe. You should be able to clearly detect some of the aromas of the bourbon. The added benefit of this method is that the aroma will stay on your hands for at least the next hour, so you can experience it again if you like.

Some knowledge of the human olfactory and gustatory senses is important here. How do people smell and taste? The brain begins to receive flavor messages as soon as we sense anything placed near the nose or on the tongue. These messages are converted into recognition of what we are smelling and tasting. The brain stores this information, and the next time one encounters the same aroma, it is familiar and detectable. The

tongue can sense six tastes: sweet, salty, sour, bitter, umami, and spicy. A study in the last decade discovered that humans can distinguish up to 1 trillion scents. With the brain storing that much information, sometimes people can become overwhelmed in seeking the correct match for what exactly they are experiencing.

**SWEET.** Sweet is the first flavor that humans detect. In the original "tongue map," the taste buds at the front and tip of the tongue are labeled sweet taste buds. Research has proven that taste bud receptors for each of the flavors are evenly distributed across the tongue, but if sweet does exist in something we taste, the tongue and brain are keen to recognize this flavor.

**SALTY.** Salt is essential to human life, which is why it is recognizable by the human tongue. For the most part salt does not play a part in tasting bourbon unless salt is used in a cocktail.

**SOUR.** Sour is acidity. A good way to detect acidity is saliva. The more acidity, the more your mouth will produce saliva. Acidity is most likely detected in bourbon cocktails that feature a citrus fruit or juice.

**BITTER.** Bitter can be unpleasant to the palate, which is why it is one of the most recognizable of flavors, but bitter can be desirable and help to balance sweet and sour flavors. Beer drinkers know hops for their bitter flavor. Gin lovers are most likely familiar with tonic water, in which the quinine adds a bitter component.

**UMAMI.** Umami is savory. This flavor was first defined by the Japanese in the early twentieth century. Umami is present in food with glutamic acid and/or high concentrations of nucleotides. Examples of these foods include meat and mushrooms.

**SPICY.** Spicy is overwhelming to the tongue and can cause a burning sensation. Peppers are usually the cause of this effect, but ethanol is also a cause.

Here a bourbon drinker swirls the bourbon. *Photo by Clay Banks*

A bourbon drinker sniffs, or *noses*, the bourbon, the most important step in the tasting process. *Oskars Kupics/Shutterstock.com*

The nose can detect and distinguish at least 1 trillion different odors. The more you taste and smell, the better you will be able to taste and smell. The more odors you are exposed to, the better you will be able to explain what you are smelling. We are going to use the mouth and nose together when tasting bourbon to maximize our experience.

There are five "S's," or steps, to tasting bourbon:

**SEE.** Look at the bourbon in the glass. The liquid should be between a medium amber and a dark golden brown color. By looking at the whiskey we can deduce several truths about the spirit. The longer a whiskey is aged in barrels, the darker it is. Newly charred barrels give a darker color to whiskey versus whiskey aged in a barrel that has previously been used. So a darker whiskey has been aged longer and/or has been aged in a newly charred barrel.

**SWIRL.** To swirl, rotate the glass of bourbon and watch. The liquid should move around the side of the glass in a small wave. Swirling the bourbon will help hidden aromas emerge for your enjoyment. At first you may only pick out one or two aromas, but perhaps in the future you will be able to identify more. However, if you never find more than a few aromas you will still be in good company.

**SNIFF**. The sniff is where a consumer becomes a connoisseur. This is the most important step in the process of tasting the bourbon because the tongue can only taste six flavors: sweet, salty, sour, bitter, umami, and spicy. The nose helps the tongue convert flavor messages from the simple to the specific. The sniff is important because it allows the drinker to enjoy the bourbon on a new level. Here you will be able to pick out aromas like vanilla, hay, caramel, butterscotch, apricot, and peach, to name a few. One hard-and-fast rule for drinkers of spirits: when you taste a spirit, be sure to keep your lips parted as you inhale the aromas of the bourbon through your nose. By doing this you will avoid inhaling alcohol vapors that will agitate or burn the nasal cavity, creating an unpleasant experience. If you want a little more information but you are having trouble distinguishing the details of a bourbon, try the trick of pouring a little bourbon into one hand and rubbing your hands together. Now wave your hands in front of your face. This should help you pick up some of the details that you missed in the glass.

**SIP**. The sip is important because it converts the theoretical flavors detected by the nose into reality on the palate.

Once the bourbon is in your mouth, a good practice is to pretend to chew the bourbon with your mouth closed. This practice is called the Kentucky chew. When you are finished, you should breathe in through your mouth and out through your nose. This will help you to pick out flavors and aromas in the bourbon.

**SAVOR**. Savoring is decision making. Once the bourbon has moved around your mouth, consider what you are tasting. What do you like about the bourbon? What flavors do you detect? What aromas? Did you experience a Kentucky hug? Take notes. Share your thoughts with friends and compare your reactions. Tasting is best done with friends because you will learn from them and they will learn from you. Aroma and flavor are both based on experience. The more you experience, the better you will be able to detect aromas and flavors. By adding people to your bourbon-tasting group, you will be able to draw from each person's experience in flavor and aroma. If you don't always agree with another person's assessment of the bourbon, that is okay because we all perceive aromas and flavors a little differently. The more you taste bourbon, the better you will become at the process and the more details you will detect. Good news! Practice makes perfect!

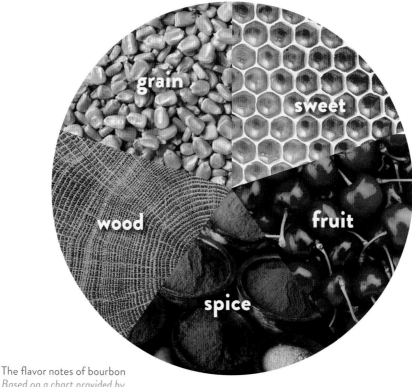

The flavor notes of bourbon
*Based on a chart provided by*
*Chris Morris/Woodford Reserve*

However, no matter how long you practice, you may still be at a loss when it comes to detecting specifics in the bourbon that you taste. This is part of the reason that Master Distiller Chris Morris created the Bourbon Flavor Wheel. People who have formally tasted wine may be familiar with the aroma wheel created by Dr. Ann Noble at the University of California, Davis. The Bourbon Flavor Wheel works in the same way with bourbon.

The wheel has five sections: grain, sweet, fruit, wood, and spice, with more specific aromas on the outside of the wheel. You should start at the center of the wheel and move to the outside as you feel comfortable to pinpoint specific aromas. To start the tasting, look at the bourbon and determine the color. Swirl the bourbon. As you begin to nose the bourbon, first try to detect the innermost part of the wheel.

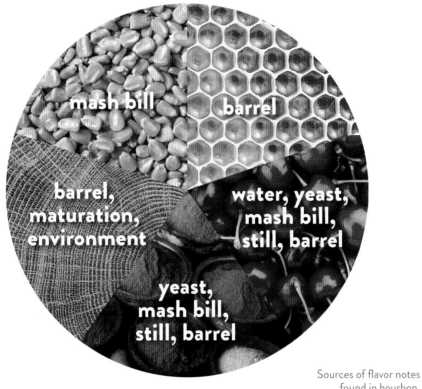

Sources of flavor notes
found in bourbon.
*Based on a chart provided by
Chris Morris/Woodford Reserve*

As you work your way to the outside of the wheel, you can get specific. Can you detect grain? If so, which grain? Corn? Rye? Wheat?

Now try to detect sweet. Is that sweet like honey? Or vanilla? Perhaps caramel or butterscotch?

Can you detect wood? Oak? How about other aromas of wood? Cedar? Walnut? Pecan?

Now look for spice. Black pepper? Mint? Clove, or perhaps cinnamon? Anise? How about coffee or tobacco?

Now look for fruits and flowers. Peach? Apricot? Orange? Cherry? Rose? Geranium?

A more complex flavor wheel
developed by Woodford Reserve.
*Based on a chart provided*
*by Chris Morris/Woodford Reserve*

The aromas that you detect come from several places. The grain aromas and flavors in bourbon come from the mash bill. You should always be able to detect corn when nosing bourbon because the mash bill is made up of mostly corn. A mash bill that is higher in rye will produce a bourbon that has a spicy rye aroma, while a mash bill that has a higher wheat content will produce a bourbon that has a sweet wheat aroma.

The wood aromas come from the barrels in which the bourbon is aged. The final aromas will vary depending on the barrel's placement in the rickhouse and the number of seasons the bourbon is aged. If the barrel is placed higher in the rickhouse, the bourbon will tend to have a pronounced wood flavor because heat rises, forcing the bourbon to interact with the barrel in a dramatic way. Bourbon placed in lower parts of the rickhouse will have less interaction with the barrel in which it is stored. Bourbon placed in other places in the rickhouse will have varying interaction with the wood barrels. Barrel placement—ultimately the microclimate in which the bourbon is placed—has a lot to do with the aromas and the flavor of the bourbon.

The sweetness in bourbon comes from two places: the alcohol, which is always sweet, and the barrel. When the cooper chars the inside of the barrel, the sugars caramelize, which explains the caramel, butterscotch, honey, and vanilla aromas. As for the coconut, chocolate, and maple syrup, the fire that caramelizes the sugars also creates a chemical compound that smells a lot like these elements in the bourbon.

The spice that is detected in bourbon comes from a combination of the yeast, the mash bill, the still, and the barrel working in four-part harmony. Some of the spices that can be detected in bourbon—not all, because the spices will change from batch to batch and from barrel to barrel—can include cinnamon, clove, nutmeg, mint, black pepper, tobacco, coffee, leather, and licorice (liquorice for my British Commonwealth friends).

The fruit and flower aromas come from a combination of the water, yeast, mash bill, the still, and the barrel. These aromas can include orange, lemon zest, apples, pears, figs, raisins, dates, apricots, cherries, berries, and bananas.

Now, time for a test! Don't panic, this is one you should enjoy: a tasting test! Generally when tasting, I like to pour about one-half to three-quarters of an ounce in each glass. Remember, this is a tasting—save the larger pours for enjoyment! Also, make sure that you have a white background, like a piece of paper, so that as you tip the glass to look at the bourbon, the color will be easy to see. You should also have a glass of water to sip in between tasting each bourbon. You may also want to include coffee beans or coffee grounds in a small cup. You will want to nose the coffee to clear or reset your olfactory receptors before you taste the next bourbon.

> **TEST #1**. Have a friend set up three glasses in no particular order but use the three bourbons that you chose and tasted in the first lesson: one classic, one high-wheat, and one high-rye bourbon. Review the tasting notes in your notebook. Have your friend pour the three glasses, keeping track of which glass

Three bourbons poured for a taste test. Can you tell which is *classic*, which is *wheated*, and which is *high rye*? *barmalini/Shutterstock.com*

holds which bourbon. Go through the formal tasting listed in this lesson. Can you pick out which is the classic, wheated, and high-rye bourbon? Keep notes on your tasting. Can you find specific aromas? Flavors?

**TEST #2**. Have a friend set up three glasses of whiskey in no particular order including a glass of bourbon, a glass of Irish whiskey, and a glass of Scotch whisky. For an ideal test each whisk(e)y should be aged the same number of years. In this scenario the darkest liquid should be the bourbon for the simple reason that it is the only whiskey in this group aged in newly charred barrels. In fact, the other two may be aged in used bourbon barrels. If the whiskeys are aged the same amount of time, the interaction between the whiskey and the newly charred wood will allow the bourbon to steal more color from the host barrel. Can you pick out the bourbon on sight? Can you pick out the bourbon by the aroma? What aromas and flavors can you pick out in each of the whiskeys?

**TEST #3**. Have a friend set up three glasses in no particular order but include a glass of four-year-old bourbon, a glass of ten-year-old bourbon, and a glass of fifteen-year-old (or older) bourbon. In this scenario the darker the liquid, the older the bourbon because the bourbon interacted with the barrel for a longer time. Can you pick out the youngest bourbon? Can you pick out the oldest bourbon? If you were mistaken, why did you pick the wrong bourbon?

Please don't waste perfectly good whiskey after these tests. You and your friend should enjoy!

If you are going to evaluate more than three or four bourbons in one sitting, I strongly suggest you consider investing in a spit bucket. Wait a second—who spits out bourbon? Spitting out perfectly good bourbon is wrong! Frankly, the only time that I propose spitting bourbon out is when you are at a large tasting. The whole point of a tasting is to enjoy the bourbon and to learn about the product. Enjoying bourbon fully is

Master Distiller Parker Beam evaluating new make. *Courtesy of Heaven Hill Distillery*

near impossible if you are intoxicated. In a small tasting, no more than three or four bourbons, or when you are at a bar, allow gravity to take the caramel liquid to your stomach. Enjoy! If you do plan to consume the bourbon, make sure that you have a designated driver.

One last consideration: your notes may look different from your friends' and they may look different from the experts'.

As I mentioned at the beginning of the chapter, some of the best advice I received on tasting bourbon came from Parker Beam. We were sampling various bourbons from Heaven Hill Distilleries. Each one of the panel members spoke to their olfactory experience with each bourbon: what they liked, what their experience was, the flavors and aromas that they were able to detect. Parker stayed mum. As we finished the tasting, one of the audience members asked to hear the master distiller's opinion of the bourbon. Parker said, "When people ask me what aromas I smell in our bourbon, I just tell them, 'It smells like bourbon to me.'" Parker's answer drew cheers and applause—indeed, a standing ovation—from the audience of culinary professionals. The master distiller had delivered the most important lesson of the day: don't overthink the bourbon—remember to enjoy it!

# QUIZ #4

**1. What is the first flavor that humans taste?**

A. Sweet

B. Sour

C. Salty

D. Bitter

E. Spicy

**2. What is the first step to tasting bourbon?**

A. See

B. Swirl

C. Sniff

D. Sip

E. Savor

3. What is the last step to tasting bourbon?

A. See

B. Swirl

C. Sniff

D. Sip

E. Savor

4. In which step in tasting should you be able to pick out aromas like vanilla, hay, caramel, and butterscotch?

A. See

B. Swirl

C. Sniff

D. Sip

E. Savor

5. A good way to detect acid is:

A. Aroma

B. Saliva

C. Bitterness

D. None of the above

6. The nose can detect and distinguish at least _____ odors.

A. 100,000

B. 1 million

C. 1 billion

D. 1 trillion

7. A darker bourbon suggests that the bourbon has been:

A. Aged longer

B. Bottled longer

C. Aged for a shorter time

D. Bottled for a shorter time

8. If evaluating more than three or four bourbons, you should:

A. Drink less

B. Drink more

C. Have a spit bucket at the ready

D. None of the above

9. A good test to pick up the aroma of bourbon is:

A. Use your hands

B. Use a towel

C. Use your feet

D. Use a plate

10. When looking for the aromas in bourbon, part your:

A. Lips

B. Hair

C. Fingers

D. None of the above

# LESSON 5

# DON'T JUDGE A BOTTLE BY THE LABEL

MAGINE TWO PEOPLE SITTING ENJOYING A GLASS OF bourbon. They're relaxed, talking about their lives, their spouses, their children, their work (but only a little) as they bond over the bourbon, and everything else melts away. I have had this experience more than once. Bourbon brings people together. But what we want to know in this scenario is: what bourbon are they drinking?

## EXPANDING HORIZONS

Some people know exactly which bourbon they are going to order every single time they sit down at the bar or which bottle they are going to pick up from the liquor store. For them the answer is always the same—and very safe. They know what they enjoy and that is what they stick with, always. You should resist the urge to stay with the safe choice. Finding the right bourbon should be all about experimentation. But how do you find the perfect bourbons for you? There are so many to choose from, and it can be overwhelming. Personally, I have never found a bourbon that I didn't like, but I do enjoy certain bourbons more than others. The key to enjoying bourbon is expanding your horizons.

Start with your friends. If they drink bourbon, what do they recommend? Perhaps they would be willing to share a glass before you invest in an entire bottle. If you exchange gifts with these friends for holidays or birthdays, you might suggest that their next gift to you be *their* favorite bourbon. Another strategy is to order bourbon at a bar but instead of ordering what you already know, try something new. Try the bourbons whose names you don't recognize. In this method you accrue the added benefit of getting the bartender's opinion. Make sure that you frame the question as something like, "I love bourbon, but I want to try a bourbon that I have not tried before. What do you think of (*fill in the blank*)?" Or, better, give the bartender the choice of two bourbons with which you are unfamiliar. Remember, the more information you share with bartenders, the better they will be able to guide you. Be willing to tell bartenders what bourbons you like (wheated? high-rye?) because that may help them to guide you to a bourbon that will maximize your enjoyment.

AlenKadr/Shutterstock.com

The Urban Bourbon Trail (see lesson 8 for details) is the perfect time and place to try this second strategy. Bartenders in Louisville (and the larger Commonwealth) pride themselves on their knowledge of bourbon. They keep up on trends and new releases, and many are personally familiar with or know the movers and shakers in the bourbon industry. Finally, you should consider traveling the Kentucky Bourbon Trail (see lesson 9). As you go from distillery to distillery, take part in the tastings at each location and ask questions. Between your friends, bartenders, the Urban Bourbon Trail, and the Kentucky Bourbon Trail, you should be able to determine which bourbons you like best.

Ask your bartender to recommend bourbons you haven't tried yet. *bogdanhoda/ Shutterstock.com*

A selection of six bourbons based on my recommended categories for stocking a personal bar.
*Courtesy of Laura Hohman*

## HOW MANY BOURBONS SHOULD YOU STOCK?

What should you stock in your personal bar? I recommend that every bourbon lover maintain a basic stock of three to six bourbons, minimum. The first three are covered by the tasting kit you assembled in lesson 1: a classic bourbon, a wheated bourbon, and a high-rye bourbon. I keep these so that when my friends stop by, I'm sure to have a bourbon they will enjoy. If you are happy with this group, you are set and ready for company. If not, you can replace individual bottles with other brands as you go along. My personal collection includes at least three other categories: a bottle for cocktails, a bottle for sipping, and a bottle for special occasions.

To be clear, my six bottles have changed over the years. I started with my father's favorite bourbon and one that Master Distiller Lincoln Henderson recommended. . . . Try to guess the brand name on that bottle. I have kept both in stock, although

A much larger collection of bourbon, but don't be intimidated. This selection is on display at the Brown Hotel in Louisville. *Rosemarie Mosteller/Shutterstock.com*

my father's favorite has increased in price and scarcity. Now that it's so hard to find and very expensive, I don't always have this bottle in my collection, but I have good substitutes that I think my father would enjoy. My collection has expanded over the years to include more than six bottles, which ensures that I always have the right bourbon for the mood—and at a moment's notice.

When you discover a bourbon you like, add it to your collection. The unexpected discovery of a new (and, more important, *good*) bourbon is one of the great joys for the bourbon enthusiast. The resolute search for new bourbons turns the bourbon enthusiast into a bourbon hunter. I suggest that you aspire to become a bourbon hunter to the extent your pocketbook and circumstances will allow. Make sure to keep notes on your tasting, and compare your notes with those of your friends. Most of all, be sure to enjoy the process, because bourbon is meant to be enjoyed.

Spirits, scotch, and whiskey aisle in a liquor store. *Mihai_Andritoiu/Shutterstock.com*

# THE UNUSUAL SUSPECTS

On a bourbon run to the local liquor store, I happened upon a bottle that would change my short-term drinking and my long-term hunting. I picked out the usual bottles: one for special occasions, one for sipping, and one for cocktails. As I approached the checkout counters, I noticed that most of my neighborhood had decided to make their liquor run on the same day, at the same time. The registers were packed with long lines. As I waited I reviewed the offerings behind the counter. All of the small pints and half bottles were lined up, facing forward as if they were waiting for a witness to identify them for the police. The usual suspects were all there—Woodford Reserve, Bulleit, Buffalo Trace, Elijah Craig, Evan Williams, Jim Beam, Knob Creek, and Maker's Mark. All of them excellent choices!

As I stood in line, I noted one bottle I was unfamiliar with—one quite unlike the recognizable suspects in the lineup. The bottle was thin and tall for a half bottle, with firm shoulders on top, reminiscent of a half bottle of Bordeaux, and its deep amber color was displayed perfectly through the silk-screened label. Spying the price (very affordable), I made the snap decision that this half bottle needed to take a ride with me and spend the rest of its life imprisoned at my home bar. My hope was that in adding a bottle to my collection I would learn something I did not already know. For me, the half bottle is a sign of quality for one of two reasons, and sometimes both: Some distilleries offer a half bottle when a whiskey is very popular and they know that any size bottle will sell. The other possible reason is that the bourbon is of such high quality or rarity that its price is high; it becomes more affordable in a half bottle. In this case the bourbon was of high quality and the price was very affordable.

Once I got it home the bottle did not last long. By the end of the week I was back to buy a full bottle, and by the end of the next month I was back to buy a 1.75-liter bottle. Soon this bourbon became my special occasion bourbon. When I first found this bourbon, a little unsure of what I had, I decanted the bottle. When I offered a glass from this decanter to visitors, I always got the same response: "Wow! This is very good bourbon! What is in your decanter?" I would smile and say, "Guess!" They would try, and the vast majority would fail.

Fast-forward fifteen years: the bourbon is a unicorn. I have a hard time keeping my collection stocked with it. It's difficult to find the 750-milliliter bottle, and I can't find the 1.75-liter bottle at all anymore. Other bourbon lovers have caught onto the value of this bourbon and now seek it out. The price has increased exponentially; when I do find the bourbon, I have to pay more than double the original price.

Another bottle that I like to stock is one that begins with the word "Old." I like this bourbon for cocktails. Anytime I am mixing bourbon with something else, I pull this bottle for use. This bottle makes wonderful Old Fashioned bourbon cocktails. It also mixes well with sweet vermouth for excellent Manhattans. For special occasions, I also make cocktails with bourbon that carries a higher price point.

I have several bottles for special occasions. One was a gift from a good friend when we finished a major project. Another was a birthday gift from my brother; he sent me a gift card with instructions to buy a bottle of bourbon that I did not own. I have a great brother! I took the opportunity to expand my horizons and bought something that I had been hoping to try for a while. The bottle was a good choice, and I made a promise to my brother that I would save some for him. That is going to be a hard promise to keep.

The most important lesson in this chapter is not to count out any bourbon just because you have not heard of it. Expand those horizons!

# QUIZ #5: A PRACTICAL EXAM

For this exam you will need to pull out your pocketbook and go to your local liquor store. Go to the bourbon section and pick up at least two bourbons with which you are unfamiliar. When you get home, complete a tasting of these bourbons. What do you think about them? How do they compare to the ones you already own? How do they compare to the bourbons you really enjoy? Are you excited about these bourbons or disappointed? Will you buy them again? Make sure to keep notes. Compare your notes to online reviews and the notes of your friends.

# LESSON 6

# HOW TO ORDER A BOURBON

T O CALL OR NOT TO CALL . . . that is the question. Should you name the bourbon you want to order or rely on the bartender or server to help you with your decision? Most bourbon experts will call out a bourbon. Many of these calls are for top-shelf bourbon. The top shelf of the bar is usually reserved for the best bourbon—or at least the rarest and most in-demand. If you don't call your bourbon, you will most likely receive bourbon from the well or the speed rack behind the bar.

# BAR LINGO

**Aperitif**: A before-dinner drink designed to stimulate the appetite. In most cases this drink will have a high acid content.

**Behind the stick**: A slang term describing the work behind a bar or the act of bartending.

**Bitters**: A flavor enhancer made from herbs, spices, and/or berries. Bitters act as seasoning for many cocktails, including the Old Fashioned and the Manhattan. The most common example stocked at a bar is Angostura bitters. Other flavors include Peychaud's bitters, orange, mint, cinnamon, chocolate, grapefruit, and celery bitters, to name a few.

**Blended**: If you want a smooth consistency, you should ask for your drink "blended" or "frozen."

**Bourbon and branch**: A term for bourbon with water. The "branch" refers to still water that has passed through limestone filtering. In Louisville and most of Kentucky, "branch" could refer to tap water, but the term originally meant water from a natural spring or tributary that flows into a larger source.

**Brut**: A term used to describe the driest French Champagne.

**Build**: A type of cocktail created in the glass in which it will be served to the customer.

**Call**: Refers to a customer using the brand name of a distilled spirit when ordering. For example, "Jim Beam on the rocks."

**Chaser**: A shot served after another drink. For example, a customer might order a beer with a bourbon chaser.

A bottle of Angostura bitters.
*Alexander Prokopenko/Shutterstock.com*

An Old Fashioned cocktail with cherries and orange peel. *Brent Hofacker/Shutterstock.com*

**Cocktail**: A generic term for a large class of mixed drinks.

**Cooler**: A drink served in a tall glass. Usually served during the summer months, this drink sometimes has alcohol added to the mixture. A Presbyterian cocktail is an example.

**Cordial**: A liqueur that is served after dinner and is known for the warming sensation it provides. Bourbon Cream is an example.

**Dash**: A measurement equal to two drops. Many times bitters are added to drinks in dashes. The Old Fashioned, the Manhattan, and the Seelbach cocktail all call for dashes of bitters in the recipe.

**Double**: A drink or cocktail made with double the amount of alcohol. If you order a double bourbon, you should expect twice the amount of alcohol to be poured into the glass. This can be served with or without ice. Not to be confused with a tall drink.

**Doux**: The French word for "sweet," used to describe sweet Champagne or sparkling wine with a lot of residual sugar.

A bartender finishing a cocktail by adding a dash of flavoring. *Maksym Fesenko/Shutterstock.com*

The cocktail technique known as *flaming*, in which the upper layer of alcohol is ignited.
*Tkachuk Iuliia/Shutterstock.com*

**Down**: For the most part this is an extinct practice. If a customer orders a "bourbon down," they should expect the bartender to deliver a bourbon that has been chilled with ice and strained into a rocks glass.

**Drop**: A bar measurement of a single drop.

**Dry (very dry)**: A bar term used to describe how much (or, more accurately, how little) vermouth is added to a Martini. A dry Martini has little vermouth added to the mix and a very dry Martini even less. This term is also used to describe a Manhattan, but in that case it refers to the type of vermouth used to create the cocktail. Someone who orders a dry Manhattan should expect it to be made with dry vermouth.

**86**: A slang term that means to discontinue service of something or to someone. There are many possibilities as to where the term originated. It may have originated in a bar in the Old West. If a customer became intoxicated, the bartender would switch the patron from 100-proof to 86-proof whiskey. Or the term could have originated in New

York, where Code 86 made it a crime for bartenders to serve intoxicated customers. Or the term may have arisen during Prohibition, relating to a speakeasy located at 86 Bedford Street in Greenwich Village, New York. If the police raided, customers would 86 themselves out of the bar. Or the term could refer to the standard depth of a grave in the United States, 86 inches. Or it might relate to the Uniform Code of Military Justice, article 86: Absent without Leave (AWOL).

**Fizz**: A cocktail that includes a carbonated base, lemon (or citrus), and sugar. A Bourbon Fizz might be a bourbon with carbonated water, orange, and sugar. A fizz is usually served with ice.

**Flaming**: A bar term used to describe the practice of igniting the alcohol on top of the drink before the cocktail is served. This practice is not allowed in all jurisdictions.

**Float**: A bar term used to describe the practice of adding an alcohol to a drink and allowing it to float to the top of the drink. Floating alcohol is possible based on the specific gravity or the relative viscosity of the two liquids. A lighter liquid can float on top of a heavier one. A customer may order a drink with a bourbon float. An example of this is the Tropical Itch cocktail.

A cocktail garnished with flowers.
*Elena Gordeichik/Shutterstock.com*

**Garnish**: A fruit, flower, herb, or spice added to a drink for color. Examples include the orange slice and cherry on top of an Old Fashioned or the cherry in a Manhattan.

**Highball**: An alcoholic drink or cocktail that is made with one liquor mixed with carbonated soda.

A cocktail served in a highball glass.
*kazu326/Shutterstock.com*

A bartender using a jigger to measure alcohol for a mixed drink. *Maksym Fesenko/Shutterstock.com*

**Jigger**: A bartender's small measuring cup. Also a measurement of 1½ ounces of liquor or distilled spirit. However, before Prohibition the term referred to a measurement of 2 ounces.

**Julep**: A sweetened alcoholic cocktail that is consumed during the day. A julep usually consists of simple syrup, a flavoring ingredient, a distilled spirit, and ice. In Kentucky, the most common is the Mint Julep, made with simple syrup, mint, bourbon, and ice. The Mint Julep is the official cocktail of the Kentucky Derby.

**Liqueur**: A sweetened distilled beverage flavored with a fruit, herb, or other flavor.

**Liquor**: A term used to generally describe a distilled spirit.

**Mist**: A term used to describe a distilled spirit served over chips of ice. If you order a bourbon mist, expect bourbon served over chips of ice, compared with a drink served "on the rocks," which indicates cubes of ice.

A classic Mint Julep cocktail—the official drink of the Kentucky Derby. *Brent Hofacker/Shutterstock.com*

A bartender releases flavor by mashing ingredients with a muddler. *Maksym Fesenko/Shutterstock.com*

**Mixer**: Any liquid added to a spirit, commonly juice, soda, or water.

**Muddle**: Mashing ingredients such as oranges or cherries for a cocktail like an Old Fashioned. A bartender uses a tool called a "muddler" to aid in muddling fruit or herbs in a drink.

**Naked**: Another term for neat.

**Neat**: Alcohol served alone in a glass. Someone who orders a "bourbon neat"

should expect a glass with about 1½ ounces of bourbon.

**Nip**: A bar term referring to the measurement of 2 ounces of distilled spirit. If someone asks for a "nip of bourbon," they are asking for 2 ounces of bourbon. This could be asked in tandem with another term, for example, "a nip of bourbon on the rocks."

**On the rocks**: Bar language for "with ice." For example, if you ask a bartender for a

A glass of bourbon served on the rocks.
*WNstock/Shutterstock.com*

**Pony**: A bar measurement equal to 1 ounce of bourbon or other spirit.

**Rickey**: A cocktail that originated in Washington, D.C., served in a highball glass consisting of bourbon or gin, lime juice, and carbonated water. A Rickey is not sweetened. The cocktail is named for Colonel Joe Rickey, a Washington lobbyist. July is Rickey month in Washington, D.C.

**Rolling a drink**: A bartender method similar to building a drink, where the ingredients are poured into a cocktail tin, then transferred to another tin and back to the original one, which thoroughly chills the drink without over-diluting it. This is a good method

"bourbon on the rocks," you should expect a short glass with at least 1 ounce of bourbon filled more than halfway with ice.

Cocktail shaker, strainer, and other tools used for preparing cocktails. *stockcreations/Shutterstock.com*

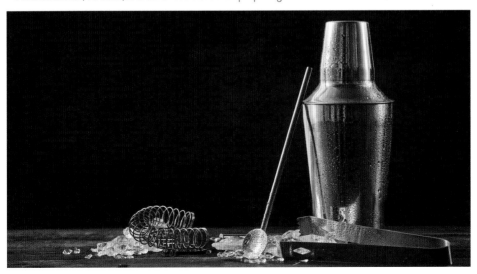

to use when over-aerating a drink is not desired.

**Sec**: A French term for "dry" that describes a sparkling wine that is off-dry or semi-sweet.

**Shake**: A bartending method where all the ingredients for a drink are poured into a cocktail tin or shaker, which is closed and shaken until the cocktail is fully chilled. The cocktail is then strained into a cocktail glass for service. Generally this method is reserved for drinks that include ingredients besides alcohol, such as juice. Bartenders often use a Boston shaker, which consists of a tin and a

16-ounce mixing glass. The tin fits over the glass and seals tight for shaking.

**Shooter**: Any combination of spirits that is served neat in a shooter or shot glass.

**Shot**: A bar term to describe 1½ ounces of a spirit served in a shot glass neat. Customers sometimes order a shot of whiskey.

**Simple syrup**: A sugar syrup made from at least equal parts sugar and water to sweeten cocktails. Simple syrup can be flavored to add another layer of complexity to a cocktail. Simple syrup is used to make the Old Fashioned and the Mint Julep.

A bottle of homemade simple syrup. *Brent Hofacker/Shutterstock.com*

A bartender stirring a cocktail. *Maksym Fesenko/Shutterstock.com*

**Sour mix**: A premade mixture kept behind the bar that is used to make many drinks, including sours. Sour mix can be homemade by the bartender using a combination of limes, lemons, oranges, sugar, water, and sometimes egg whites.

**Splash**: A small amount of liquid that is more than a dash but less than ½ teaspoon.

**Sprinkle**: A small amount of liquid that is less than a dash, or about ⅙ of a teaspoon. The term is usually used in a bar.

**Stir**: A bartending method where the ingredients are poured into a mixing glass with ice. The mixture is then stirred with a long bar spoon until it is fully chilled, then is strained into a chilled glass. This method is usually used when all of the ingredients in a cocktail are alcoholic, such as in the Manhattan.

A bartender pours a cocktail through a strainer. *Maksym Fesenko/Shutterstock.com*

**Straight up**: Refers to a spirit that is quickly chilled, then strained into an empty glass. Someone who orders a bourbon straight up should expect the bartender to pour bourbon into a mixing glass, add ice, stir the bourbon until chilled, then strain the bourbon into an empty glass. This method allows the bourbon to be chilled and diluted without continued dilution throughout the process.

**Strain**: Refers to a bartender separating the liquid in a cocktail from the ice using a strainer. This process happens with most cocktails that are stirred or shaken.

**Swizzle**: A cocktail made with crushed ice is stirred with a device called a swizzle stick. The cocktail is usually stirred until the glass becomes frosty.

**Tablespoon**: A kitchen and bar measurement equal to ½ fluid ounce or 3 teaspoons.

**Tall**: A drink served in a tall glass with more mixer to fill the glass. Generally ordered by the customer as a way to enjoy a cocktail longer without the negative effects of alcohol. Not to be confused with a double.

**Teaspoon**: A kitchen and bar measurement equal to four dashes or two splashes of liquid.

A Hot Toddy cocktail with lemon, cinnamon sticks, and star anise.
*Brent Hofacker/Shutterstock.com*

**Toddy**: A hot cocktail prepared by mixing liquor with hot water and a sweetener such as honey or sugar. The recipe can also include lemon slices and spices such as cinnamon or cloves. Traditionally an evening drink, especially favored when the person consuming it has a cold or the flu.

**Up**: A distilled spirit is served "up" when the bartender chills the spirit with ice before straining it into a glass. Traditionally, an "up" drink is served in a cocktail glass or martini glass, which stands higher than a rocks glass or an Old Fashioned glass—thus "up."

**Wineglass**: As a measurement in old cocktail books, a full wineglass equals about 6 ounces. Sometimes these older bar texts require a wineglass full of a liquid, other times half a wineglass of a liquid ingredient, or 3 ounces.

**With a simple mixer**: A drink served with a mixer and ice, for example, bourbon with Coke. The customer should expect bourbon served over ice and topped with the mixer.

**With a twist**: A cocktail with a citrus zest strip. For example, a customer may ask for a "bourbon with an orange twist." The customer should expect a glass of bourbon (on the rocks, straight up or neat) served with an orange twist.

**With water**: A spirit served watered down, for example, bourbon with water. There should not be so much water that it changes the flavor of the bourbon.

A Boulevardier cocktail served on the rocks with an orange twist. *Micaela Fiorellini/Shutterstock.com*

A toast! *L.O.N Dslr Camera/Shutterstock.com*

# HERE IS A TOAST FOR YOU!

While living in Louisville, I had the pleasure of being a member of Skål, an organization composed of travel and tourism professionals, including hotel general managers, travel agents, cruise executives, airline executives, executive directors for county tourism boards, restaurant managers, facilitators of bourbon-related experiences, and others who provide service to travelers and tourists. Every month the local chapter of Skål held a membership meeting at one of the city's restaurants. Toward the scheduled end of the board meeting, held before the general meeting, all members of the group would arrive early at the bar for friendship, fellowship, and a drink. We would socialize and discuss many things—families, basketball, and bourbon among them. When the board meeting was over, the board members would join everyone else at the bar before we all moved to the dining room. We would enjoy a three- or four-course meal, including a glass of wine. A short business meeting about Skål affairs was held during dinner. The evening meeting always began with a member offering a toast to the rest of the group, who would then repeat it: Good health! *Good health!* Friendship! *Friendship!* Long life! *Long life!* Happiness! *Happiness!* Skål! *SKÅL!* Then someone in the group would add an unofficial Y'all! And others would join in, *Y'all!*

One rule was followed during the evening: no business! A person's individual business could not be discussed during the meeting. The most one could do was offer a later phone call, something like, "I'll call you tomorrow." One of the reasons I enjoyed my time with SKÅL was because the group focused on friendship. When you picked up the phone to ask someone for a favor, the person at the other end was always glad to help because they were your friend. The toast at the end of the SKÅL-related business meeting, usually held between courses, was a very classy way to remind everyone why they were attending.

Anyone who goes to the bar to celebrate an occasion should have a few toasts ready to celebrate the person or people being honored. Here are a few toasts that you can use or adapt. From a simple toast to a more complex one, each will be appreciated by friends.

## SIMPLE TOASTS

Arabic: *Belsalamati Kah-sahk* (Your cup)

Chinese: *Gān bēi* (Cheers)

Danish: *Skål* (Cheers)

French: *À votre santé* (To your health)

Gaelic: *Slainte* (Health)

German: *Prost* (Cheers)

Hawaiian: *Hauoli maoli oe*
(To your happiness)

Hebrew: *L'chaim* (Health)

Italian: *Cin cin* (Cheers)

Japanese: *Kanpai* (Dry cup)

Norwegian: *Skål* (Cheers)

Portuguese: *A sua saude* (To your health)

Russian: *Za vas* (To you)

Spanish: *Salud* (Health)

Swedish: *Skål* (Cheers)

## FOR FRIENDSHIP

Four blessings upon you: older bourbon, younger (wo)men, faster horses, more money!

A toast to ships! There are good ships and wood ships and ships that sail at sea, but here is to the best ships, friendships—may they always be.

## FOR AN ANNIVERSARY

To the lovely couple: proof that love, like bourbon, improves with time.

## FOR PROMOTIONS

To a well-deserved award for a job well done.

## FOR RETIREMENT

Love, health, money, and time to enjoy them!

## FOR BIRTHDAYS

A toast to your coffin. May it be of one-hundred-year oak. And may we plant the tree together tomorrow.

Age is something that doesn't matter, unless you are bourbon!

## FOR WEDDINGS

May your love be as endless as your wedding rings!

To the luckiest (wo)man on earth . . . and the (wo)man who made him/her that way!

# QUIZ #6

**1. If you want a chilled bourbon served without ice, you should ask for it to be served:**

A. Down

B. Up

C. Sideways

D. None of the above

**2. If you want a bourbon served over ice, you should ask for it served:**

A. Straight

B. Mist

C. On the rocks

D. Down

**3. When a liquid is added to a spirit, it is referred to as:**

A. Neat

B. Nip

C. Naked

D. A mixer

**4. Which of the following drinks is muddled?**

A. Bourbon and Coke

B. Manhattan

C. Old Fashioned

D. Toddy

**5. Which of the following drinks is stirred?**

A. Bourbon and Coke

B. Manhattan

C. Old Fashioned

D. Toddy

**6. When you want twice the amount of alcohol in your mixed drink, you should ask for it:**

A. Tall

B. Doux

C. Double

D. Down

**7. Naming the bourbon you want in your glass or used in your cocktail is referred to as a:**

A. Well

B. Build

C. Call

D. Drop

**8. Wishing people well during a special occasion is called:**

A. A toast

B. An aperitif

C. A chaser

D. A cordial

**9. A fruit, flower, herb, or spice added to a drink for color is referred to as:**

A. Fizz

B. Float

C. Garnish

D. Nip

**10. Which of the following refers to a drink served without ice?**

A. Neat

B. Up

C. Down

D. All of the above

# LESSON 7

# BOURBON COCKTAILS

WHILE BOURBON LOVERS MAY ENJOY THEIR FAVORITE SPIRIT without a mixer, bourbon is also brilliant in cocktails. The Old Fashioned, the Manhattan, and other classics are the perfect prelude to a meal with friends or family, and they are also a great way to end the evening. Generally, you should use your "cocktail bourbon" for cocktails, but I have several bourbons that straddle the line between cocktail and sipping bourbon; they function well as both.

The granddaddy of all cocktails is the Old Fashioned. While this cocktail can be made with any spirit, whiskey is most commonly used. For those who favor bourbon, no other spirit will do for the Old Fashioned. According to bourbon lore, the cocktail was developed at Louisville's Pendennis Club because bourbon producers wanted to create a market for their spirit. A bourbon Old Fashioned is one of my favorite cocktails. Angostura bitters are most commonly used by bartenders for this drink. Your first Old Fashioned should be made with Angostura bitters, but you should experiment with other bitters to find your favorite cocktail flavors. I usually combine Angostura bitters and Peychaud's bitters in equal parts. As for choice of bourbon, use your favorite bourbon at a middle to low price point. The only time to use top-shelf bourbon would be for a very special occasion—although some would argue that top-shelf bourbon should only be enjoyed without additives. When I wrote *The Old Fashioned: An Essential Guide to the Original Whiskey Cocktail*, my research led me to the conclusion that fruit was not part of the original composition of this cocktail. This is great news for the many bourbon aficionados who prefer the drink without the muddled fruit.

One day I walked into Equus and Jack's Lounge, a restaurant in St. Matthews, Kentucky, which is in Louisville's Metro area. I sat at the bar, hoping to enjoy an amazing cocktail prepared by 2016 Bourbon Hall of Fame inductee, bartender, and author Joy Perrine. Perrine had become a friend during our frequent speaking gigs about bourbon. She spotted me down the bar and immediately started working on a drink. In a minute she arrived where I was sitting, put down a napkin, and placed an Old Fashioned on top. She looked me square in the eye and said, "Hey, kid, you said that muddled fruit was optional. Drink this and tell me it isn't the best Old Fashioned that you ever had." Then she walked away to tend to her other customers. Perrine was right! She had delivered a wonderful cocktail. In her book, *The Kentucky Bourbon Cocktail Book,* coauthored with Susan Reigler, the Old Fashioned is the first cocktail listed in the "Classics" chapter; she offers up a stellar version of the cocktail that features muddled fruit and a heavy-handed dose of bitters. You can adapt the recipe below by muddling the fruit in the glass before you add the ice.

# THE OLD FASHIONED

¼ **ounce simple syrup**

**2–6 dashes bitters**

**2 ounces bourbon**

**Orange slice**

**Cocktail cherry**

Pour the simple syrup into the bottom of an Old Fashioned glass followed by the bitters. Add ice to the glass and stir. Add the bourbon and stir again. Garnish with an orange slice and a cocktail cherry. As noted above, some choose to muddle the fruit.

In his book *Everyday Drinking,* British novelist Sir Kingsley Amis referred to the Manhattan as "the not very energetic man's Old Fashioned," calling it "an excellent drink." Sir Kingsley also expressed in no uncertain terms that the use of bourbon for this cocktail and the Old Fashioned is non-negotiable. A classic Manhattan includes 100% sweet vermouth, a dry Manhattan uses 100% dry vermouth, and the "perfect Manhattan" features both vermouths in equal parts. The bitters component is a good place to experiment with this drink. As for bourbon, make sure to use a middle to top-shelf bourbon. The Manhattan is traditionally made with an American whiskey. Some people prefer rye whiskey, but a high-rye bourbon works well for this cocktail.

## THE PERFECT MANHATTAN

**2 ounces bourbon**

**½ ounce sweet vermouth**

**½ ounce dry vermouth**

**2 dashes bitters**

**Cocktail cherry**

**Orange twist**

Add ice and water to a cocktail glass to chill the glass. Add ice in a mixing glass. Then add the bitters, bourbon, sweet vermouth, and dry vermouth and stir at least forty times. Empty the ice from the cocktail glass, add the cherry to the bottom of the glass, and strain the contents of the mixing glass into the cocktail glass. Twist the orange over the glass and lightly wipe the outer rim with the orange twist before adding it to the drink.

The Perfect Manhattan. *Brent Hofacker/Shutterstock.com*

The Mint Julep. *Wollertz/Shutterstock.com*

Another cocktail that must be made with bourbon is the Mint Julep. The festive Mint Julep is the official drink of the Kentucky Derby, easy to make and enjoy. To those who say they don't like Mint Juleps, I ask you to try one more before casting final judgment on this cocktail. First, pick a top-quality bourbon; second, make sure you don't crush your mint; and finally, don't be in a rush to finish the cocktail—Juleps are to be sipped and savored. Also, I think it helps to drink Juleps when the mint is fresh and in season.

# THE MINT JULEP

**¼ ounce simple syrup**

**4–6 mint leaves**

**2–3 ounces bourbon**

**Mint sprig**

Add the simple syrup to a pewter or silver julep cup. Lay the leaves out on your palm and lightly smack them with your other hand. Add them to the cup. Add the bourbon and mix. Then add crushed ice. Smack the mint sprig between your hands and add to the julep as a garnish.

There is a plethora of hotels in downtown Louisville. Al Capone enjoyed staying at the historic Seelbach Hotel, which also inspired F. Scott Fitzgerald's Mulbach Hotel in *The Great Gatsby*. The Seelbach Hotel provides a good central location from which to enjoy the many bourbon-themed attractions in the area. If you visit the Seelbach Hotel, make sure to visit the Rathskeller in the hotel's basement and the bar located off the lobby at ground level. Order the hotel's signature cocktail, the Seelbach.

## THE SEELBACH COCKTAIL

**7 dashes Angostura bitters**

**7 dashes Peychaud's bitters**

**1 ounce bourbon**

**½ ounce Cointreau**

**4 ounces Champagne**

**Lemon twist**

Add ice to a mixing glass. Then add the bitters, bourbon, and Cointreau. Stir until cold. Strain into a sparkling wine flute and add the Champagne until full. Garnish with the lemon twist.

A good way to wake up the palate at the end of a busy day is a nice Bourbon Sour. This cocktail should be consumed before dinner. For a sour you want to make sure that you are using a good bourbon, one that you like, so you maximize your enjoyment of this drink, because the bourbon will shine in this cocktail.

# THE BOURBON SOUR

**1½ ounces bourbon**

**1 ounce lemon juice**

**½ ounce simple syrup**

**¼–½ ounce egg whites**

**Dash bitters**

**Orange slice**

**Cocktail cherry**

Add ice and water to a cocktail glass or a rocks glass to chill the glass. Add ice to the tin side of a Boston shaker. In the mixing glass, add Angostura bitters, bourbon, lemon juice, simple syrup, and egg white. Pour the contents of the mixing glass into the iced tin and secure the glass to the tin. Shake the contents until the ice sounds different and the contents are cold. Open the Boston shaker. Empty the cocktail or rocks glass (and refill it with ice if you prefer to drink a whiskey sour on the rocks), then strain the contents of the shaker into the glass. Garnish with an orange slice and cocktail cherry.

The Bourbon Sour. *Marian Weyo/Shutterstock.com*

The origin of the Bourbon Cobbler is lost to history, but this cocktail is wonderful on a late spring or summer day. The muddled fruit adds acidity and sweetness to this drink, making the Cobbler refreshing.

# THE BOURBON COBBLER

**1 pineapple slice**

**1 orange slice**

**1 lemon slice**

**2 ounces bourbon**

**½ ounce orange Curaçao**

**Mint sprig, to garnish**

Add the pineapple slice, orange slice, and lemon slice to the bottom of a rock glass or an Old Fashioned glass. Gently muddle the fruit, extracting the juices. Add the bourbon and orange Curaçao to the glass and stir. Add ice to the drink. Take the mint sprig in one hand and clap your hands together to release the oils in the mint. Add the mint to the top of the drink for garnish.

The Boulevardier is the perfect before-dinner drink. The bitterness of the Campari helps to prepare the palate for a meal. This drink is very similar to the Negroni, a gin-based drink.

## THE BOULEVARDIER

**1½ ounces bourbon**

**1 ounce sweet vermouth**

**1 ounce Campari**

**Orange twist**

Add all of the ingredients into a rocks or Old Fashioned glass. Add ice and the orange twist.

The Boulevardier. *Maksym Fesenko/Shutterstock.com*

Lemonade is the perfect drink for a hot summer's day. The bright, cold flavor of the lemons is tasty and refreshing. The only way to improve this is by adding a little bourbon to the mix.

## LOUISVILLE LEMONADE

**2 lemon wedges**

**2 teaspoons superfine sugar**

**2 ounces bourbon**

**Lemon-flavored soda**

Muddle the lemon and sugar together in a highball glass. Add ice to the top, bourbon, and lemon-flavored soda to top off. Stir gently.

The Presbyterian. *Brent Hofacker/Shutterstock.com*

The Presbyterian Church (PCUSA) is a result of the reunification of the United Presbyterian Church in the United States of America (UPCUSA) with the Presbyterian Church in the United States (PCUS). The two churches separated in 1861 as a result of the Civil War: UPCUSA was the church of the northern states and PCUS was the church of the southern states. The Civil War ended in 1865, but the two churches didn't reunite until 1983. The headquarters of UPCUSA was in New York City while PCUS headquarters was in Atlanta. As the two churches merged, they chose Louisville as their new national headquarters. The City of Louisville made the move extremely attractive by offering to sell PCUSA a large building in downtown Louisville for $1. While the creation of this cocktail predates the merger of the two churches, everyone, northern and southern, can agree that the Presbyterian is a great drink.

# THE PRESBYTERIAN

**1½ ounces bourbon**

**2 ounces club soda**

**2 ounces ginger ale**

**Ice**

Fill a highball glass with ice. Add the bourbon, then the club soda and ginger ale. Stir.

Every year the Boy Scouts of America hold capital campaigns at the local council level. The hope is to raise money for the Boy Scouts to continue their mission of training Scouts. Scouting has always been a part of my life. My grandfather was an Eagle Scout, my great-uncle was a scouting executive in Kansas City, I am an Eagle Scout, and both of my sons were Scouts: the eldest, Thomas, completed a 110-mile trek to Philmont, and the younger, Michael, completed his Eagle. I am always glad to help out the scouting cause. One of the Boy Scout executives, John Cary, asked if I would create a signature cocktail for the capital campaign. Yes, Scouts drink bourbon too! The CEO of Brown-Forman was spearheading the fundraising that year (2010, the hundredth anniversary of scouting), so I created the BSA using one of the company's liqueurs, Southern Comfort (now owned by the Sazerac Company).

## THE BSA

**1 ounce Woodford Reserve Bourbon**

**1 ounce Southern Comfort**

**3 ounces Ale-8-One**

In a rocks glass add ice. Pour in the Woodford Reserve, add the Southern Comfort, and top with Ale-8-One. Gently stir. Enjoy!

The Hot Toddy is a wonderful cold-weather cocktail, traditionally an evening drink.

# THE HOT TODDY

**5 whole cloves**

**1 lemon slice**

**2 ounces bourbon**

**1 ounce lemon juice**

**1 tablespoon honey or simple syrup**

**2½ ounces hot water**

**Cinnamon stick**

Place a heatproof glass on your work surface. Secure the cloves on the lemon slices by pushing them into the lemon peel. This will be used as part of the garnish. Add the lemon juice to the glass, followed by the hot water and honey or simple syrup. Stir the mixture until well incorporated. Add the bourbon and stir. Add the lemon garnish and the cinnamon stick to the cocktail.

A Hot Toddy. *Liv friis-larsen/Shutterstock.com*

Another Kentucky industry is horse racing and all the cultural celebration that implies. The neck of a horse is very important because in a close race that is what determines the winner at the finish line. Make sure to include your favorite bitters and favorite bourbon for maximum enjoyment.

## THE HORSE'S NECK

**1½ ounces bourbon**

**4 ounces ginger ale**

**1 dash bitters**

**Lemon twist**

Add ice to a highball glass. Add the bitters, bourbon, and ginger ale. Stir gently and garnish with a long lemon twist.

The Horse's Neck. *Wirestock Creators/Shutterstock.com*

Arnaud's Restaurant is located on Bienville Street just off Bourbon Street in New Orleans's French Quarter. The restaurant was founded in 1918 by Count Arnaud Cazenave. This cocktail is very similar to the Sazerac but made with bourbon instead of rye, and this cocktail is not sweetened.

# ARNAUD'S SPECIAL

**1 dash Peychaud's bitters**

**1 dash Angostura bitters**

**2 ounces bourbon**

**2 dashes absinthe**

**Lemon twist**

Add ice to an Old Fashioned glass. Add the bitters, bourbon, and absinthe and then stir. Add more ice if needed. Stir again. Twist the lemon twist over the top of the glass and rub against the rim. Add the twist to the drink.

A commodore is a senior captain in the navy and coast guard. While use of this rank is for the most part outdated in the United States, many other navies still use the term for a sailor who holds the rank above captain and below rear admiral. Enjoy this cocktail with a mid-tier bourbon.

# THE COMMODORE

**1½ ounces bourbon**

**¾ ounce white crème de cacao**

**½ ounce lemon juice**

**¼ ounce grenadine**

**2 dashes bitters**

Add ice and water to a cocktail glass to chill the glass. Place the bourbon, white crème de cacao, lemon juice, grenadine, and bitters in a Boston shaker with ice and shake until the mixture is cold. Pour out the ice and water in the cocktail glass. Strain the mixture into the glass. Garnish with a lemon twist.

As the Commonwealth of Kentucky is landlocked, people more often associate another military rank that starts with "C" with Kentucky. The Kentucky Colonel commission is the highest award given by the governor of Kentucky. Once someone is granted a commission as a colonel, they can use that title, serve as an "aide-de-camp" to the governor, and be eligible for membership in the Honorable Order of Kentucky Colonels, which exists to "aid and promote the Commonwealth and its citizens," raising funds to do "good works" all over the Commonwealth.

## THE KENTUCKY COLONEL

**2 ounces bourbon**

**½ ounce Benedictine liqueur**

**1 dash of orange bitters**

**1 dash of Angostura bitters**

**Ice**

**Lemon twist**

Add ice and water to a cocktail glass to chill the glass. Place the bitters, bourbon, and Benedictine liqueur in a Boston shaker with ice and shake until the mixture is cold. Pour out the ice and water in the cocktail glass. Strain the mixture into the glass. Garnish with a lemon twist.

The Brown Hotel is a historic hotel in Louisville. When you visit you must try the Hot Brown, a turkey, bacon, tomato, and Mornay sauce–covered sandwich that is broiled to a bubbly golden brown. You can order chef Fred Schmidt's culinary creation in one of the hotel's restaurants or at the bar, which is located in the lobby up a beautiful staircase from street level. If you choose the bar, you should also order the Brown's signature cocktail, named for Louisville's favorite son, 1960 Olympic gold medalist and boxing heavyweight champion of the world Muhammad Ali. The Brown's version is made with agave nectar and sometimes rye, but mine gives a nod to the bees with the use of honey. Ali used to say, "I float like a butterfly and sting like a bee!"

# THE MUHAMMAD ALI SMASH

**1 ounce honey**

**1 ounce PAMA liqueur**

**1 ounce bourbon**

**1 lemon wedge**

**6 mint leaves**

**Crushed ice**

Muddle the lemon wedge with the fresh mint leaves and honey, then add the liquors and crushed ice.

# QUIZ #7

1. The Old Fashioned has which of the following?

A. Bourbon

B. Bitters

C. Sugar

D. All of the above

2. The Perfect Manhattan has which of the following?

A. Bourbon

B. Sweet vermouth

C. Dry vermouth

D. All of the above

3. Which of the following cocktails is the official drink of the Kentucky Derby?

A. Old Fashioned

B. Mint Julep

C. Manhattan

D. Louisville Lemonade

4. Which of the following cocktails is created with a sparkling wine?

A. Old Fashioned

B. Mint Julep

C. Seelbach

D. Manhattan

5. Which of the following cocktails was created at the Brown Hotel?

A. Old Fashioned

B. Muhammad Ali Smash

C. Louisville Lemonade

D. Boulevardier

6. Which of the following cocktails is similar to the gin-based Negroni?

A. Manhattan

B. Boulevardier

C. Seelbach

D. Old Fashioned

7. Which of the following drinks is made with equal parts club soda and ginger ale?

A. Presbyterian

B. Boulevardier

C. Manhattan

D. Louisville Lemonade

8. Which of the following cocktails is made with egg whites?

A. Old Fashioned

B. Boulevardier

C. Bourbon Sour

D. All of the above

**9. Which of the following cocktails is made with white crème de cacao?**

A. Bourbon Sour

B. Kentucky Colonel

C. Commodore

D. Louisville Lemonade

**10. Which of the following cocktails features mint in the recipe?**

A. Mint Julep

B. Bourbon Cobbler

C. Muhammad Ali Smash

D. All of the Above

# LESSON 8

# FOOD PAIRING WITH BOURBON AND THE URBAN BOURBON TRAIL

THE BOURBON CLASSIC IS LOUISVILLE'S FOOD AND BOURBON event of the year. For me, the highlight of the long weekend is the Cocktail and Culinary Challenge, featuring competition by two-person teams—a chef and a bartender. Each team is sponsored by a bourbon brand. The goal is to impress the panel of judges, as well as the attendees, with food and cocktails in two categories: "Classic Cocktails" with a small plate and "Contemporary Cocktails" with a small plate. The chefs and the bartenders pull out all the techniques and tricks of their trades to blow away the judges. At the end of the competition, awards are given out based on the judges' selections of Best Team in Classic, Best Team in Contemporary, Best Culinary Classic, Best Cocktail Classic, Best Culinary Contemporary, and Best Cocktail Contemporary, and the audience chooses the recipient of the People's Choice Award for Cocktail and Culinary. That's right, the judges are not the only people assessing the offerings!

During a four-year span from 2014 to 2017, I served as a judge for the Cocktail and Culinary Challenge competition at the Bourbon Classic. I loved judging this challenge for several reasons, but primarily because the cocktails are always amazing, and the small plates are delicious. Every team brought its best recipes, both cocktail and culinary. One of the hard parts for me was that many of the bartenders had become friends during my years in Louisville, and many of the chefs were former students. But everyone adhered

to the highest professional standards, and these friendships have endured. I was honored to serve as a judge alongside some of the best and brightest of Louisville's culinary scene.

Looking back, I am struck by how much I learned through this experience. The chefs, even my former students—especially my former students—showcased techniques and recipes that were flawless. The team I was a part of at Sullivan University had completed our mission: our students took what we taught them and built on that knowledge. The bartenders showcased the versatility of bourbon as a cocktail ingredient, proving that it can be used in all of the classics, of course—the Old Fashioned, the Manhattan, the Mint Julep—and also as a base for delicious new cocktails born of their creativity.

Every year when I returned home from the event, I did not have to eat for a day because I had exceeded my caloric intake for the entire week. I had fun and learned so much from judging.

## BOURBON WITH FOOD—AND IN FOOD!

How do you go about picking foods that pair well with bourbon? Bourbon has a big flavor, so the trick is to find a food that also has a big flavor, so that the bourbon does not completely overpower the food. At the same time you want a food that will enhance your enjoyment of the bourbon. Once you have picked your bourbon, there are two approaches: complement the food or contrast the food. There are a couple more rules you will want to keep in mind. Avoid spicy food! The alcohol will accentuate the spice in the food. Look for proteins with fat and sweets.

Cooking with bourbon is easy, but make sure you use the bourbon in moderation so that it does not overpower the food. Think of bourbon as a spice for your food, an ingredient you will want to use sparingly.

If you are new to using bourbon as a cooking ingredient, there are ways to develop your technique. For starters, look at your favorite recipes. Where can bourbon be added? You can substitute bourbon for the alcohol in almost any recipe, and with brilliant results. Bourbon is an excellent substitute for vanilla in baking recipes, and it can replace brandy in any recipe. The trick is to not use too much bourbon.

Lastly, be sure to cook with a bourbon that you like to drink but also one that is not going to break the budget.

Bourbon can often be substituted for vanilla extract in baking recipes. *New Africa/Shutterstock.com*

A historical plaque in downtown Louisville informing passersby about Evan Williams, Kentucky's first distiller. *4kclips/Shutterstock.com*

# THE URBAN BOURBON TRAIL

Visitors to Louisville can also take part in the city's Urban Bourbon Trail® (UBT). The UBT will take you all over Louisville and, as a bonus, introduce you to some of the best food in the region. A digital passport can be downloaded by following the links at www.bourboncountry.com. After reviewing the list of restaurants and pubs, pick your top six, visit, check in, and you will qualify for an Urban Bourbon Trailblazer T-shirt.

### BOURBON'S BISTRO

2255 Frankfort Avenue, Louisville, Kentucky 40206; http://bourbonsbistro. com/; 502-894-8838

### BUCK'S RESTAURANT

425 West Ormsby Avenue, Louisville, Kentucky 40203; https://www.buckslou. com/; 502-637-5284

### CORNER RESTAURANT & BAR

102 West Main Street, Louisville, Kentucky 40202; https://www. cornerlouisville.com/; 502-583-1888

### DERBY CAFÉ AT THE KENTUCKY DERBY MUSEUM—704 Central

Avenue, Louisville, Kentucky 40208; https://www.derbymuseum.org/; 502-637-1111

This barrel sculpture and an interpretive sign designate Fourth and Main Streets as the center of the Bourbon District in Louisville. *Rosemarie Mosteller/Shutterstock.com*

### DOC CROW'S SOUTHERN SMOKEHOUSE & RAW BAR

127 West Main Street, Louisville, Kentucky 40202; https://www.doccrows.com/; 502-587-1626

### 8UP ELEVATED DRINKERY & KITCHEN—350 West Chestnut Street, Louisville, Kentucky 40202; https://www.8uplouisville.com; 502-631-4180

### GARAGE BAR—700 East Market Street, Louisville, Kentucky 40202; https://www.garageonmarket.com/; 502-749-7100

### HARRODS CREEK TAVERN

6313 River Road, Louisville, Kentucky 40059; https://www.harrodscreektavern.com/; 502-919-8812

The Galt House, home of Jockey Silks Bourbon Bar. *4kclips/Shutterstock.com*

**JOCKEY SILKS BOURBON BAR**—140 North Fourth Street, Louisville, Kentucky 40202 (second floor of the West Tower of the Galt House); https://www.jockeysilksbourbonbar.com/; 502-566-3205

**LOBBY BAR & GRILL AT THE BROWN HOTEL**—335 West Broadway, Louisville, Kentucky 40202; https://www.brownhotel.com/dining/lobby-bar; 888-888-5252

**MERLE'S WHISKEY KITCHEN**—122 West Main Street, Louisville, Kentucky 40202; https://merleswhiskeykitchen.com/; 502-290-8888

**THE OLD SEELBACH BAR**—500 South 4th Street, Louisville, Kentucky 40202; http://www.seelbachhilton.com/dining; 502-585-3200

**PROOF ON MAIN**—702 West Main Street, Louisville, Kentucky 40202; https://www.proofonmain.com/; 502-217-6360

**RECBAR**—10301 Taylorsville Road, Jeffersontown, Kentucky 40299; https://www.recbarlouisville.com/; 502-509-3033

A banner declaring the Louisville Bourbon District the "Birthplace of Bourbonism."
*Rosemarie Mosteller/Shutterstock.com*

A sign at Sway Restaurant at the Hyatt Regency Louisville designates it as the first stop on the Urban Bourbon Trail. *Rosemarie Mosteller/Shutterstock.com*

**RIVER HOUSE RESTAURANT AND RAW BAR**—3015 River Road, Louisville, Kentucky 40207; https://www.riverhouselouisville.com/; 502-897-5000

**ROC**—1327 Bardstown Road, Louisville, Kentucky 40204; https://www.rocrestaurant.com/; 502-459-7878

**SIDEBAR AT WHISKEY ROW** 129 North 2nd Street, Louisville, Kentucky 40202; 502-630-2012

**SWAY**—320 West Jefferson Street, Louisville, Kentucky 40202; https://www.hyatt.com/en-US/hotel/kentucky/hyatt-regency-louisville/sdfrl/dining; 502-581-1234

The Troll Pub Under the Bridge, located on the site of the original Galt House hotel, serves lunch and dinner as well as local bourbons. *Rosemarie Mosteller/Shutterstock.com*

**TAJ LOUISVILLE**—807 East Market Street, Louisville, Kentucky 40206; 877-825-6858

**TROLL PUB UNDER THE BRIDGE**
150 West Washington Street, Louisville, Kentucky 40202; https://www.trollpub.com/louisville/; 502-618-4829

**21ST IN GERMANTOWN**
1481 South Shelby Street, Louisville, Kentucky 40217; https://www.21stgermantown.com/; 502-654-7221

**WHISKEY DRY**—412 South 4th Street, Louisville, Kentucky 40202; https://www.4thstlive.com/eat-and-drink/whiskey-dry-by-ed-lee; 502-749-7933

Be sure to check the websites of these restaurants and bars before you visit. Restaurants sometimes move, sometimes close, and sometimes are no longer participating members of the trail. I would hate for you to make the effort to visit these locations only to find out that the restaurant you picked is no longer open or is no longer part of the trail!

Lastly, when you are out drinking bourbon, it is also important to drink *water*. Please stay hydrated, remember to eat, and enjoy bourbon responsibly.

# QUIZ #8

The experience of taking the Urban Bourbon Trail *is* the exam, an externship of sorts. The T-shirt you receive at the end of the trail shows that you passed the quiz with honors. The T-shirt also gives you bragging rights to your friends who have not traveled the trail.

# LESSON 9

# THE KENTUCKY BOURBON TRAIL AND THE AMERICAN WHISKEY TRAIL

FOR BOURBON LOVERS, A PILGRIMAGE TO KENTUCKY IS obligatory because most bourbon, about 95% of the world's supply, is produced in the Bluegrass State. Plus, the Commonwealth has a rich history surrounding America's native spirit. Many whiskey pilgrims use Louisville as their "base camp" while venturing out on the Camino of Bourbon. Bourbon pilgrims may fly into Louisville International Airport or drive into the city via I-64 (running east and west) or I-65 (running north and south). The two highways intersect in the downtown area like an X on a map marking the location of a great golden treasure—or, in this case, a great amber treasure. The corporate headquarters of many companies that produce bourbon are sited at this crossroads.

Downtown Louisville is a great base for a bourbon pilgrimage. Moving south to north, 4th Street features several historic hotels: the Brown at 4th and Broadway, the Seelbach at 4th and Muhammad Ali, and the Galt House at 4th Street overlooking the Ohio River. These hotels are known for their unique architectural features, and each is within walking distance of world-class restaurants and bars. In addition, visitors to the Brown can enjoy the iconic Hot Brown sandwich invented in the hotel kitchens in 1926 by Chef Fred K. Schmidt. The Brown has an incredible bar in the ornate lobby. Visitors to the Seelbach can enjoy the marble-clad lobby, the incredible staircase, the historic Rathskeller, and the fabled bourbon-based Seelbach cocktail, served in the

Louisville's skyline overlooking the Ohio River. *Sean Pavone/Shutterstock.com*

Louisville's famous hot brown sandwich. *Rosemarie Mosteller/Shutterstock.com*

The Galt House, a Trademark Collection Hotel, features beautiful waterfront views. *Hendrickson Photography/Shutterstock.com*

world-class bar right off the lobby. When guests enter the Seelbach Hotel, they will understand why it was a favorite of F. Scott Fitzgerald and Al Capone. Visitors to the Galt House have a choice between several bourbon-themed bars, including Jockey Silks Bourbon Bar, Down One Bourbon Bar, and Swizzle, which is perched on top of one of the two towers of the Galt House and features unforgettable views of the Ohio River.

If you are coming from out of state, consider flying into Louisville International Airport (SDF). You never know who will be on that flight. You might be sitting next to a bourbon expert or a master distiller. Undoubtedly you will be seated near someone who lives in the Louisville area, and these are the people to ask for recommendations on where to eat, what places to visit, and what activities to include in your trip. For the most part, Kentuckians are friendly and proud of their Commonwealth.

One time I was flying home to Louisville, and my connection was at the Cincinnati/ Northern Kentucky International Airport. On the short flight I was sitting next to a nice man with a German accent. He told me that he, his brothers, and their father had come from Hamburg to follow the Bourbon Trail to fulfill their father's bucket-list dream. As the miles evaporated behind us, I told the family what I am about to share with you.

This bronze statue of philanthropist James Graham Brown, cast by Raymond Graf, stands in front of the landmark Brown Hotel, which Brown funded and built in 1923.
*Rosemarie Mosteller/Shutterstock.com*

Flying back to Louisville from Washington, D.C., I had the unexpected pleasure to sit next to fellow author and bourbon expert Michael Veach (right).

The *Kentucky Bourbon Trail Passport & Field Guide* allows you to keep track of your bourbon journey. *Courtesy of the Kentucky Distillers' Association*

I was amazed that a family would travel from Germany to visit the world headquarters of bourbon. When the son sitting next to me asked about my occupation, he was excited to learn that I had written a book about cooking with bourbon. It was a book the family had to own. Luckily, it was for sale at the Louisville Airport, so they started their trip with a signed copy. For me, this interaction confirmed the worldwide reach of bourbon—this distilled beverage is nothing less than an international force!

# THE KENTUCKY BOURBON TRAIL

The Kentucky Bourbon Trail is a food and beverage tourism trail that connects bourbon enthusiasts with the people and places related to the industry. A bourbon pilgrim can begin in Louisville, following the trail by taking I-65 south to the Clermont exit to visit the Jim Beam Distillery. Alternatively, the bourbon devotee can travel east on I-64 toward Lexington, to begin the Bourbon Trail.

The information included here is accurate at the time of publication, but with time the master distillers will change to a new guard, and the ownership of the distilleries may change as large corporations buy and sell brands.

## THE DISTILLERIES ON THE TRAIL

**ANGEL'S ENVY**. As you begin your journey on the bourbon trail, you don't have to travel far to visit one of the top distilleries producing bourbon. Angel's Envy Distillery is located in downtown Louisville. A young distillery, Angel's Envy only dates back to 2010, with their first release in 2011. The distillery was founded by Master Distiller Lincoln Henderson and his son Wes Henderson. Angel's Envy employs many members of the Henderson family in key positions. The elder Henderson was instrumental in creating Woodford Reserve and Gentleman Jack for Brown-Forman and was honored as one of the inaugural inductees into the Kentucky Bourbon Hall of Fame. The younger Henderson is credited with talking his father out of retirement to start Angel's Envy and with continued innovation with the brand since his father's death in 2013. In 2019, Wes Henderson joined his father in the Kentucky Bourbon Hall of Fame.

Angel's Envy distillery in downtown Louisville. *Courtesy of the Kentucky Distillers' Association*

The dining room at Bardstown Bourbon Company. *Courtesy of the Kentucky Distillers' Association*

Bulleit Bourbon distillery. *Courtesy of the Kentucky Distillers' Association*

The distillery is known for aging bourbon in "finishing barrels," after the usual aging process, to provide added complexity. Angel's Envy produces a port-finished bourbon, rum-finished rye, cask strength port-finished bourbon, an oloroso sherry-finished bourbon, and tawny port-finished bourbon.

**BARDSTOWN BOURBON COMPANY.** When you travel to Bardstown, Nelson County, take in the Bardstown Bourbon Company, which claims the honor of being the first Napa Valley–style destination on the trail. John Hargrove and Steve Nally are the master distillers.

**BULLEIT BOURBON.** Located in Lebanon, Marion County, and Shelbyville, Shelby County. The Bulleit brand was introduced in 1830 by Augustus Bulleit and then later reintroduced in 1987 by his great-great grandson, Tom Bulleit. The Bulleit brand is owned by Diageo.

Evan Williams Bourbon Experience. *Rosemarie Mosteller/Shutterstock.com*

**EVAN WILLIAMS BOURBON EXPERIENCE.** Sited on Whiskey Row in downtown Louisville, this attraction features an amazing tour that takes the bourbon enthusiast on a trip back in time to an experience that chronicles the origins of bourbon, the period of Prohibition, and modern-day bourbon. The experience includes a working small still. The Evan Williams Bourbon Experience is owned by Heaven Hill Distilleries, whose master distiller is Conor O'Driscoll.

**FOUR ROSES.** Located in Lawrenceburg, Anderson County. The master distiller is Brent Elliott. Four Roses is owned by Kirin Brewery Company of Japan.

Four Roses distillery. *Courtesy of the Kentucky Distillers' Association*

Green River distillery. *Courtesy of the Kentucky Distillers' Association*

**GREEN RIVER.** Located in Owensboro, Daviess County. The Green River Distillery's master distiller is Jacob Call, whose father and grandfather worked at Jim Beam. His father learned distilling from Booker Noe and later was the master distiller at Florida Caribbean Distilleries.

The visitor center at Heaven Hill distilleries. *Courtesy of the Kentucky Distillers' Association*

**HEAVEN HILL VISITOR CENTER.** Located in Bardstown, Nelson County, the Heaven Hill Visitor Center has wonderful tours of the rickhouses and a great gift shop. The visitor's center has several educational galleries, including the Bourbon 101 exhibit, the Bottled-in-Bond exhibit, Five Brothers Bar, a tasting room, a distillery theater, and a Heaven Hill family gallery.

**JIM BEAM.** Jim Beam is one of the most recognizable and best-selling brands of bourbon in the world. Based in Clermont, Bullitt County, the company has a history of producing and selling whiskey since 1795. They also have an Urban Stillhouse, a small still in downtown Louisville. Today, the distillery sells a wide range of products, from 80 proof (40% ABV) to about 129 proof (64.5% ABV). Products include straight bourbon, premium bourbons, ryes, a white whiskey, various liqueurs, and Beam's small-batch collection. The brand's production historically boasts seven generations of Beam family involvement in the production of this bourbon, including current master distillers Fred Noe and his son Freddie Noe.

**LUX ROW.** Located in Bardstown, Nelson County, Lux Row is responsible for Ezra Brooks, Lux Row, Rebel Yell, and Blood Oath, to name a few. They are proud to be, as they claim, "one of the top USA-based independent producers of alcoholic beverage." John Rempe is the master distiller.

On the grounds of Jim Beam distilleries. *Courtesy of the Kentucky Distillers' Association*

Lux Row distillery. *Courtesy of the Kentucky Distillers' Association*

**MAKER'S MARK.** Located in Loretto, Marion County. Maker's Mark Whisky is a wheated bourbon that was introduced in 1958 by the Samuels family and is known for not using rye in the mash bill. Maker's Mark bottles have a distinctive hand-dipped red wax seal at the top that drips down the neck of the bottle. Maker's Mark products have expanded in recent years to include Maker's Mark (90 proof or 45% ABV), a cask strength bourbon, Maker's 101 proof, Maker's 46, which is oak stave–finished, a wood-finished series, and a private selection. The master distiller is Denny Potter. The brand is now owned by Beam Suntory.

**MICHTER'S.** Michter's Fort Nelson Distillery is located in downtown Louisville. Michter's produces bourbon, rye, and American whiskey. Their bourbon products include a straight bourbon at 91.4 proof (45.7% ABV), a 10-year bourbon at 94.4 proof (47.2% ABV), a 20-year bourbon at 114.2 proof (57.1% ABV), and a 25-year bourbon at 116.2 proof (58.1% ABV) as well as similar rye products. The master distiller is Dan McKee.

The gift shop at Michter's. *Courtesy of the Kentucky Distillers' Association*

Exhibits on display at Old Forester Distilling Company. *Courtesy of the Kentucky Distillers' Association*

**OLD FORESTER DISTILLING COMPANY.** Based in Louisville. "The First Bottled Bourbon™" is listed at the top of their label. Several bourbons are made, including Old Forester 86 proof, 100 proof, several single-barrel bourbons, and several commemorative bourbons as well as several rye whiskeys. The "master taster" for Old Forester is Jackie Zykan, and Old Forester is under the direction of Master Distiller Chris Morris. Old Forester falls under the Brown-Forman umbrella of brands, which includes Woodford Reserve, Jack Daniels, and Finlandia Vodka, to name a few.

**RABBIT HOLE.** Located in Louisville, Rabbit Hole Distillery was founded in 2012 with a "forward-looking" mission regarding bourbon and whiskey and a willingness to experiment. Rabbit Hole produces three bourbons and a rye. The Cavehill brand is a wheated, four-grain bourbon at 95 proof (47.5% ABV), Heigold brand is a high-rye bourbon at 95 proof (47.5% ABV), and the Dareringer brand is a sherry cask–finished bourbon at 93 proof (46.5% ABV). The founder and whiskey maker is Kaveh Zamanian.

The entrance to Stitzel-Weller distillery. *Courtesy of the Kentucky Distillers' Association*

Town Branch distillery. *Courtesy of the Kentucky Distillers' Association*

The grounds of Wilderness Trail distillery. *Courtesy of the Kentucky Distillers' Association*

**STITZEL-WELLER.** Based in Louisville, Stitzel-Weller is responsible for the brands Blade and Bow and I. W. Harper. Blade and Bow is at 92 proof (46% ABV) and has a 22-year expression. The I. W. Harper brand is at 82 proof (41% ABV), while the 15-year expression is at 86 proof (43 ABV). They also have a line of "Orphan Barrels," including old bourbons ranging from 15 to 26 years.

**TOWN BRANCH.** Located in Lexington, Fayette County. Their brand list includes a bourbon, a rye, a gin, malt whiskeys, and a sherry-finished bourbon, to name a few. The master distiller is Mark Coffman.

**WILDERNESS TRAIL.** Based in Danville, Boyle County. Their list includes several bourbons, among them a 6-year-old, a bottled-in-bond, and small-batch releases as well as a rye and a vodka. The master distiller is Shane Baker.

Wild Turkey distillery. *Courtesy of the Kentucky Distillers' Association*

**WILD TURKEY.** Based in Lawrenceburg, Anderson County, Wild Turkey is a division of the Italian Campari Group. Some of the Wild Turkey brands include Wild Turkey 81, Wild Turkey 101, Rare Breed, Kentucky Spirit, Longbranch, Master's Keep, and Russell's Reserve. The master distillers are Jimmy Russell and Eddie Russell.

**WOODFORD RESERVE.** As the name suggests, Woodford Reserve Bourbon is produced in Versailles (pronounced VER-sails), Woodford County. Brown-Forman introduced the brand in 1996 with products that have a proof level of 86.4–90.4 (43.2%–45.2% ABV). The Woodford Reserve Distillery is located at the historic site of the Old Oscar Pepper Distillery, which later became the Labrot & Graham Distillery, where distilling began in 1812. The distillery is listed on the National Register of Historic Places and is designated as a National Historic Landmark. Woodford Reserve is the lead sponsor of the Kentucky Derby and is the official bourbon of the event, whose official title is "The Kentucky Derby presented by Woodford Reserve." Each year Woodford Reserve releases a unique bottle to celebrate the event. Attendees can purchase a $1,000 Mint Julep made with Woodford Reserve, with the proceeds benefiting charitable causes. The more moderately priced Mint Juleps are made with Old Forester, another bourbon owned by Brown-Forman. Chris Morris is the master distiller of Woodford Reserve, and Elizabeth McCall is the assistant master distiller.

# BOURBON TRAIL "CRAFT TOUR"

If you're interested in a small or craft distillery tour, you might also try:

**THE BARD**—Graham

**BARREL HOUSE**—Lexington

**BLUEGRASS**—Lexington

**BOONE COUNTY**—Boone County

**BOUNDARY OAK**—Radcliff

**CASEY JONES**—Radcliff

**CASTLE & KEY**—Frankfort

**COPPER & KINGS**—Louisville

**DUELING GROUNDS**—Franklin

**HARTFIELD & COMPANY**—Paris

**JAMES E. PEPPER**—Lexington

**JEPTHA CREED**—Shelbyville

**KENTUCKY ARTISAN**—Crestwood

**KENTUCKY PEERLESS**—Louisville

**LIMESTONE BRANCH**—Lebanon

**LOG STILL**—Gethsemane

**MB ROLAND**—Pembroke (Christian County)

**NEELEY FAMILY**—Sparta

**NEW RIFF**—Newport

**OLD POGUE**—Maysville

**PRESERVATION**—Bardstown

**SECOND SIGHT SPIRITS**—Ludlow

**WILLETT**—Bardstown

# THE AMERICAN WHISKEY TRAIL

Once you have traveled the Kentucky Bourbon Trail, if you want to continue your "studies" on bourbon and American whiskey, you might consider a journey on the American Whiskey Trail. You can begin the trail wherever you like, but note that the George Washington Distillery in Mount Vernon, Virginia, is considered the "gateway" to the trail. There is some overlap between the Kentucky Bourbon Trail and the American Whiskey Trail, so you can decide to either revisit some locations or move on to those that you have not seen yet.

**ALLEGANY MUSEUM**—Cumberland, Maryland

**ANGEL'S ENVY**—Louisville, Kentucky

**BARTON 1792 DISTILLERY**—Bardstown, Kentucky

**BRADFORD HOUSE MUSEUM**—Washington, Pennsylvania

**BUFFALO TRACE**—Frankfort, Kentucky

**BULLEIT FRONTIER WHISKEY EXPERIENCE**—Louisville, Kentucky

**FOUR ROSES**—Lawrenceburg, Kentucky

**FRAUNCES TAVERN MUSEUM**—Manhattan, New York

**GADSBY'S TAVERN MUSEUM**—Alexandria, Virginia

**GEORGE DICKEL**—Tullahoma, Tennessee

**GEORGE WASHINGTON'S DISTILLERY**—Mount Vernon, Virginia

**HIGH WEST**—Wanship, Utah

**JACK DANIEL'S**—Lynchburg, Tennessee

**JIM BEAM AMERICAN STILLHOUSE**—Clermont, Kentucky

**JIM BEAM URBAN STILLHOUSE**—Louisville, Kentucky

**MAKER'S MARK**—Loretto, Kentucky

**OLD FORESTER**—Louisville, Kentucky

**OLIVER MILLER HOMESTEAD**—South Park, Pennsylvania

**OSCAR GETZ MUSEUM OF WHISKEY HISTORY**—Bardstown, Kentucky

**O. Z. TYLER**—Owensboro, Kentucky

**SMOOTH AMBLER**—Maxwelton, West Virginia

**TOWN BRANCH**—Lexington, Kentucky

**WEST OVERTON VILLAGE & MUSEUMS**—Scottsdale, Pennsylvania

**WIGLE WHISKEY**—Pittsburgh, Pennsylvania

**WILD TURKEY**—Lawrenceburg, Kentucky

**WOODFORD RESERVE**—Versailles, Kentucky

**WOODVILLE PLANTATION**—Bridgeville, Pennsylvania

# BEYOND THE TRAILS

Once you have traveled the Kentucky Bourbon Trail and the American Whiskey Trail, you might consider visiting some other distilleries. Here is a list of small distilleries beyond the trail.

## COLORADO

**BRECKENRIDGE**—Breckenridge

**GOLDEN MOON**—Golden

## HAWAII

**KŌLOA RUM COMPANY**—Kalaheo

## IOWA

**MISSISSIPPI RIVER**—LeClaire

## ILLINOIS

**FEW SPIRITS**—Evanston

**KOVAL**—Chicago

## INDIANA

**STARLIGHT**—Borden

## KENTUCKY

**COPPER & KINGS AMERICAN BRANDY**—Louisville

**LIMESTONE BRANCH**—Lebanon

**MICHTER'S**—Louisville

## MAINE

**WIGGLY BRIDGE**—York

## MARYLAND

**LYON RUM**—St. Michaels

## MICHIGAN

**TRAVERSE CITY WHISKEY**—Traverse City

## MONTANA

**HEADFRAME SPIRITS**—Butte

## NEW YORK

**BLACK BUTTON**—Rochester

**FINGER LAKES**—Burdett

**NEW YORK DISTILLING COMPANY**—Brooklyn

## OHIO

**CLEVELAND WHISKEY**—Cleveland

## PENNSYLVANIA

**EIGHT OAKS CRAFT**—New Tripoli

**PHILADELPHIA DISTILLING**—Philadelphia

## SOUTH CAROLINA

**RATIONAL SPIRITS**—North Charleston

## TENNESSEE

**NELSON'S GREEN BRIER**—Nashville

**TENN SOUTH**—Lynnville

## UTAH

**DENTED BRICK**—Salt Lake City

**HIGH WEST**—Wanship

## VERMONT

**APPALACHIAN GAP**—Middlebury

**MAD RIVER**—Warren

## VIRGINIA

**CATOCTIN CREEK**—Purcellville

## WASHINGTON, DISTRICT OF COLUMBIA

**ONE EIGHT**

## WEST VIRGINIA

**SMOOTH AMBLER SPIRITS**—Maxwelton

## WISCONSIN

**GREAT LAKES**—Milwaukee

**YAHARA BAY**—Madison

# QUIZ #9

Time for another practical exam! Your job is to visit a bourbon distillery. This does not mean you have to visit Kentucky—unless you insist. Ask questions about the process and taste the whiskey (and be sure to bring your notebook).

# LESSON 10

# CONTINUING YOUR BOURBON EDUCATION

POWER COMES IN NUMEROUS FORMS. Sir Francis Bacon, 1st Viscount of St. Alban, coined the phrase "Knowledge is power" in his 1597 book *Meditationes Sacrae*. The more you know, the better your decisions. I tell my students there is no such thing as a "stupid question." The stupid question is the one you don't ask. When you are a student, it is expected that you are still learning and it is healthy to ask questions.

However, when you are billed as a "bourbon expert," asking a question you should already know the answer to does lead to some strange looks. Once I was sitting next to Fred Noe, the seventh-generation master distiller at Jim Beam. We were at a book signing—he was signing his book, *Beam, Straight Up: The Bold Story of the First Family of Bourbon,* and I was signing *The Kentucky Bourbon Cookbook.* Fred is easy to talk to and a very personable and friendly guy. We had shared the stage several times and were familiar with each other, so I felt comfortable talking with him. As I admired his book, I noted that Kid Rock—*the* Kid Rock, Robert James Ritchie—had written the foreword to Fred's book. I am a fan of Kid Rock. I looked at Fred and asked a stupid question: "How did you get *Kid Rock* to pen your foreword?" Fred cocked his head to the side and looked at me like I didn't get it. He didn't have to say a word. The easiest way to get a rock star to write your foreword is to be a rock star. Fred Noe is a rock star.

I realized then that I had been operating in a world of rock stars. All of the master distillers from all of the bourbon distilleries are rock stars. What they produce receives

Time for some bourbon and reading . . . about bourbon. *natu/Shutterstock.com*

as much "airtime" and sometimes more than the songs rock stars create. Their product, bourbon, is always in demand and never goes out of style. How did you get Kid Rock to write the foreword? Stupid question. I should have known the answer.

# FURTHER READING

The premise and goal of this book is to start you on your journey, which is what a book or a class titled "101" should do. The journey does not end here. There are many other books by amazing authors who can add more information and round out your knowledge of bourbon. Here are a few:

*Beam, Straight Up: The Bold Story of the First Family of Bourbon,* by Fred Noe with Jim Kokoris. Published by John Wiley and Sons in 2012. With a foreword by Kid Rock.

*The Birth of Bourbon: A Photographic Tour of Early Distilleries,* by Carol Peachee. Published by the University Press of Kentucky in 2015 with a foreword by Jim Gray, who was at the time the mayor of Lexington, Kentucky. Peachee provides a visual "narration" of the workings of a distillery.

*Bourbon Curious: A Tasting Guide for the Savvy Drinker, with Tasting Notes for Dozens of New Bourbons,* 2nd ed., by Fred Minnick. Published by the Harvard Common Press in 2019. Minnick is on my short list for future induction into the Kentucky Bourbon Hall of Fame.

*Bourbon Empire: The Past and Future of America's Whiskey,* by Reid Mitenbuler. Published by Penguin Books in 2015.

*Bourbon Justice: How Whiskey Law Shaped America,* by Brian Haara. Published by Potomac Books in 2018. The book features a foreword by Fred Minnick.

*Bourbon, Straight: The Uncut and Unfiltered Story of American Whiskey,* by Charles K. Cowdery. Published in 2004 by Made & Bottled in Kentucky. Cowdery is a 2009 Kentucky Bourbon Hall of Fame member.

*Bourbon: The Rise, Fall, and Rebirth of an American Whiskey,* by Fred Minnick. Published by Voyageur Press in 2016, the book features a foreword by celebrity chef Sean Brock.

*Bourbon: The Story of Kentucky Whiskey,* by Clay Risen. Published by Ten Speed Press in 2021.

*Bourbon Whiskey, Our Native Spirit: Sour Mash & Sweet Adventures,* by Bernie Lubbers. Published in 2011 by Blue River Press. The book has a foreword by Master Distiller Fred Noe. Lubbers worked for the Jim Beam Distillery before his current position with Heaven Hill Distilleries. He is known as the Whiskey Professor.

*Buffalo, Barrels & Bourbon: The Story of How Buffalo Trace Distillery Became the World's Most Awarded Distillery,* by F. Paul Pacult. Published by Wiley in 2021. F. Paul Pacult is a 2003 inductee into the Kentucky Bourbon Hall of Fame.

*How to Be a Bourbon Badass,* by Linda Ruffenach. Published by Red Lightning in 2018 with a foreword by Master Distiller Pamela Heilmann of Michter's Distillery. Ruffenach is the founder of Whisky Chicks, a group of female whiskey enthusiasts. The book explores ways to use bourbon in cocktails and food.

*The Kentucky Bourbon Cocktail Book,* by Joy Perrine and Susan Reigler. Published by the University Press of Kentucky in 2009. This book is a cocktail lover's dream, featuring tips and tricks by Joy Perrine, who was a master bartender and 2016 inductee into the Kentucky Bourbon Hall of Fame.

*The Kentucky Bourbon Cookbook,* by Albert W. A. Schmid. Published by the University Press of Kentucky in 2010, this book, arranged by season, explores ways to use bourbon in cooking and has a chapter on bourbon cocktails. The book features a foreword by the father of southwestern cuisine, Kentucky native Chef Dean Fearing. The book won the 2010 Gourmand Award for Best Cooking with Drinks Book in the World.

*Kentucky Bourbon Country: The Essential Travel Guide,* by Susan Reigler. First published by the University Press of Kentucky in 2013, this book is now available in an updated 3rd edition (2020) and is a must for anyone traveling the Kentucky Bourbon Trail. Reigler provides many details about the trail that can't be found in any other book. She is on my short list for future induction into the Kentucky Bourbon Hall of Fame.

*Kentucky Bourbon Whiskey: An American Heritage,* by Michael Veach. Published by the University Press of Kentucky in 2013. Veach provides a concise history of bourbon. Veach is a 2006 inductee into the Kentucky Bourbon Hall of Fame.

*The Kentucky Mint Julep,* by Colonel Joe Nickell. Published by the University Press of Kentucky in 2003, the book includes a section on the Kentucky Bourbon Trail.

*The Manhattan Cocktail: A Modern Guide to the Whiskey Classic,* by Albert W. A. Schmid. Published by the University Press of Kentucky in 2015, this book features a foreword by Master Mixologist Bridget Albert.

*The Manhattan Cocktail: The Story of the First Modern Cocktail,* by Philip Greene. Published by Stirling Epicure in 2016. The foreword is by Master Mixologist Dale DeGroff, a 2005 inductee into the Kentucky Bourbon Hall of Fame.

*More Kentucky Bourbon Cocktails,* by Joy Perrine and Susan Reigler. Published by the University Press of Kentucky in 2016, this book is a continuation of the authors' 2009 book with more recipes for cocktail lovers.

*The Old Fashioned: An Essential Guide to the Original Whiskey Cocktail,* by Albert W. A. Schmid. Published by the University Press of Kentucky in 2013, this book features a foreword by IACP's 2012 Sommelier of the Year John Peter Laloganes.

*The Old Fashioned: The Story of the World's First Classic Cocktail, with Recipes and Lore,* by Robert Simonson. Published by Ten Speed Press in 2014.

*Pappyland: A Story of Family, Fine Bourbon and Things That Last,* by Wright Thompson. Published by Penguin Press in 2020.

*The Social History of Bourbon,* by Gerald Carson. Published by the University Press of Kentucky in 2010 with a foreword by Michael Veach, a 2006 inductee into the Kentucky Bourbon Hall of Fame.

*Splash of Bourbon—Kentucky Spirit: A Cookbook,* by David Dominé. Published by McClanahan in 2010, this book explores ways to use bourbon in cooking.

*Which Fork Do I Use with My Bourbon?* by Peggy Noe Stevens and Susan Reigler. Published by South Limestone, an imprint of the University Press of Kentucky. The book features a foreword by Fred Minnick. Stevens is a 2019 inductee into the Kentucky Bourbon Hall of Fame.

*Whiskey Lore's Travel Guide to Experiencing Kentucky Bourbon: Learn, Plan, Taste, Tour,* by Drew Hannush. Published by Amazon in 2020.

*Whiskey Women: The Untold Story of How Women Saved Bourbon, Scotch and Irish Whiskey,* by Fred Minnick. Published by Potomac Books in 2013.

# RESPECT BOURBON'S POWER

A person walks into a bar. . . . Many jokes told among friends begin with this premise. Yet drinking is a serious undertaking fraught with grave danger for those who are not careful. Always have a safe way home or a designated driver to make sure that you get back home without hurting someone else, property, or yourself. Remember that drinking bourbon is a privilege.

Stan Lee, the iconic creator of Spider-Man, developed what has become known as the Peter Parker Principle: "With great power comes great responsibility." The more you know, the more you need to act responsibly. When you are drinking, make sure you have arranged a way to move from one place to another without putting yourself or others in danger. If you are drinking at home, make sure that you stay there. These guidelines apply to friends who are drinking with you. If you are out at a bar or on a bar crawl, make sure that you are with friends and that someone is the designated driver.

Acceptable blood alcohol content (BAC), the level of alcohol concentration in the blood, is set by state law. Currently in the United States, each state has set the BAC limit at .08%. Some states are considering a lower level. Also, each state exacts different penalties for driving while intoxicated (DWI) or driving under the influence (DUI). Most states have enhanced penalties for people who are caught with higher BAC levels, such as .14%. In some cases, the .08% limit can be reached after just a few drinks. Tables 1 and 2 list approximate BAC levels based on weight and drinks consumed. Remember: it is possible to be legally intoxicated without feeling intoxicated.

**Table 1.** BAC levels for men according to weight (in pounds) and number of drinks

|      | 0    | 1    | 2    | 3    | 4    | 5    | 6    | 7    | 8    |
|------|------|------|------|------|------|------|------|------|------|
| 100  | .00% | .04% | .08% | .11% | .15% | .19% | .23% | .26% | .3%  |
| 120  | .00% | .03% | .06% | .09% | .12% | .16% | .19% | .22% | .25% |
| 140  | .00% | .03% | .05% | .08% | .11% | .13% | .16% | .19% | .21% |
| 160  | .00% | .02% | .05% | .07% | .09% | .12% | .14% | .16% | .19% |
| 180  | .00% | .02% | .04% | .06% | .08% | .11% | .13% | .15% | .17% |
| 200  | .00% | .02% | .04% | .06% | .08% | .09% | .11% | .13% | .15% |
| 220  | .00% | .02% | .03% | .05% | .07% | .09% | .10% | .12% | .14% |

*Note:* One drink is defined as 1 ounce of 100-proof or 1.25 ounces of 80-proof liquor, 5 ounces of table wine, or 12 ounces of beer. You can subtract .01% for every 40 minutes of drinking.

**Table 2.** BAC levels for women according to weight (in pounds) and number of drinks

|      | 0    | 1    | 2    | 3    | 4    | 5    | 6    | 7    | 8    |
|------|------|------|------|------|------|------|------|------|------|
| 90   | .00% | .05% | .10% | .15% | .20% | .25% | .30% | .35% | .40% |
| 100  | .00% | .05% | .09% | .14% | .18% | .23% | .27% | .32% | .36% |
| 120  | .00% | .04% | .08% | .11% | .15% | .19% | .23% | .27% | .30% |
| 140  | .00% | .03% | .07% | .10% | .13% | .16% | .19% | .23% | .26% |
| 160  | .00% | .03% | .06% | .09% | .11% | .14% | .17% | .20% | .23% |
| 180  | .00% | .03% | .05% | .08% | .10% | .13% | .15% | .18% | .20% |
| 200  | .00% | .02% | .05% | .07% | .09% | .11% | .14% | .16% | .18% |

*Note:* One drink is defined as 1 ounce of 100-proof or 1.25 ounces of 80-proof liquor, 5 ounces of table wine, or 12 ounces of beer. You can subtract .01% for every 40 minutes of drinking.

And now we conclude with a final exam to test all the knowledge you have acquired in previous lessons. Good luck!

# FINAL EXAM

**1. Which of the following bourbons is considered a "classic" recipe?**

A. Ancient Age

B. Elijah Craig

C. Maker's Mark

D. Pappy Van Winkle

**2. Which of the following bourbons is considered a "wheated" bourbon?**

A. W. L. Weller

B. Knob Creek

C. Woodford Reserve

D. Bulleit

**3. Which of the following bourbons is considered a "high-rye" bourbon?**

A. Baker's

B. Old Fitzgerald

C. Elmer T. Lee

D. Breckenridge

**4. A bourbon that is hard to find might be referred to as a:**

A. Goat

B. Unicorn

C. Elephant

D. Donkey

**5. A small-batch bourbon is defined as:**

A. 5 barrels

B. 100 barrels

C. 1,000 barrels

D. There is no legal definition for the term

**6. Your tasting kit should include which of the following items?**

A. A notebook

B. Clear glasses

C. A classic bourbon

D. All of the above

**7. Bottled-in-bond is bottled at what proof?**

A. 80

B. 90

C. 100

D. Cask strength

**8. A barrel maker is referred to as a:**

A. Bung

B. Congener

C. Cooper

D. Dram

**9. An age statement defines what about the bourbon in the bottle?**

A. The highest age

B. The lowest age

C. An average age

D. None of the above

**10. What is the evaporation of whiskey in the barrel referred to as?**

A. Backset

B. Angel's share

C. Devil's cut

D. Feints

**11. When tasting bourbon, smelling the bourbon is referred to as:**

A. Nosing

B. Feints

C. Expression

D. Flipper

**12. A liquor store that sells prize bourbons at or near retail price is referred to as:**

A. Honey barrel

B. Honey hole

C. Angel's share

D. Flipper

**13. What is the most desirable part of the distillation?**

A. Heads

B. Hearts

C. Tails

D. Underbelly

**14. The rickhouse is:**

A. Also known as a honey hole

B. A warehouse where bourbon is stored

C. Cooperage

D. None of the above

15. The word handcrafted on the label indicates:

A. Good workmanship

B. Authenticity

C. A misleading statement

D. Nothing legally

16. Bourbon must be made in:

A. Kentucky

B. The United States

C. Bourbon County, Kentucky

D. Anywhere in the world

17. What city is known as the "Capital of Bourbon"?

A. Louisville, Kentucky

B. New Orleans, Louisiana

C. Bardstown, Kentucky

D. Frankfort, Kentucky

18. The Eighteenth Amendment to the United States Constitution limited all of the following except:

A. Production

B. Transportation

C. Selling

D. Consumption

19. The "proof" of a whiskey is the alcohol by volume:

A. Doubled

B. Tripled

C. Quadrupled

D. None of the above

20. Before the Whiskey Rebellion, who suggested a tax on whiskey to Congress?

A. George Washington

B. Alexander Hamilton

C. Thomas Jefferson

D. James Madison

21. Who said, "I have never in my life seen a Kentuckian who didn't have a gun, a pack of cards, and a jug of whiskey"?

A. George Washington

B. Alexander Hamilton

C. Andrew Jackson

D. James Madison

22. During Prohibition organized crime made money with which of the following?

A. Speakeasies

B. Bootlegging

C. Both of the above

D. None of the above

23. Which president drank a shot of bourbon every morning with breakfast?

A. Franklin D. Roosevelt

B. Andrew Jackson

C. Harry S. Truman

D. George Washington

24. Which of the following amendments to the Constitution of the United States is the only one to repeal another amendment?

A. Eighteenth

B. Nineteenth

C. Twentieth

D. Twenty-First

25. According to law, what makes up most of the mash for bourbon?

A. Corn

B. Wheat

C. Rye

D. Barley

26. Bourbon must be bottled at what proof minimum?

A. 80

B. 90

C. 100

D. 120

27. Bourbon must be aged in which of the following?

A. Oak container

B. Cherry wood barrel

C. Stainless steel

D. Concrete

28. Bottled-in-bond must always be bottled at what proof?

A. 80

B. 90

C. 100

D. 120

29. To be labeled "straight bourbon," the whiskey in the bottle must be aged at least:

A. Two years

B. Four years

C. Five years

D. Six years

30. Bourbon must not be distilled to more than what proof?

A. 125

B. 140

C. 150

D. 160

31. What is the first flavor that humans taste?

A. Sweet

B. Sour

C. Salty

D. Bitter

E. Spicy

32. What is the first step to tasting bourbon?

A. See

B. Swirl

C. Sniff

D. Sip

E. Savor

33. What is the last step to tasting bourbon?

A. See

B. Swirl

C. Sniff

D. Sip

E. Savor

34. In which step in tasting should you be able to pick out aromas like vanilla, hay, caramel, and butterscotch?

A. See

B. Swirl

C. Sniff

D. Sip

E. Savor

35. A good way to detect acid is:

A. Aroma

B. Saliva

C. Bitterness

D. None of the above

36. The nose can detect and distinguish at least _____ odors.

A. 10,000

B. 100,000

C. 1 million

D. 1 billion

E. 1 trillion

37. A darker bourbon suggests that the bourbon has been:

A. Aged longer

B. Bottled longer

C. Aged for a shorter time

D. Bottled for a shorter time

**38. If evaluating more than three or four bourbons, you should:**

A. Drink less

B. Drink more

C. Have a spit bucket at the ready

D. None of the above

**39. A good test to pick up the aroma of bourbon is:**

A. Use your hands

B. Use a towel

C. Use your feet

D. Use a plate

**40. When looking for the aromas in bourbon, part your:**

A. Lips

B. Hair

C. Fingers

D. None of the above

**41. If you want a chilled bourbon served without ice, you should ask for your bourbon served:**

A. Down

B. Up

C. Sideways

D. None of the above

**42. If you want a bourbon served over ice, you should ask for your bourbon served:**

A. Straight

B. Mist

C. On the rocks

D. Down

**43. A liquid added to a spirit is referred to as:**

A. Neat

B. A nip

C. Naked

D. A mixer

**44. Which of the following drinks is muddled?**

A. Bourbon and Coke

B. Manhattan

C. Old Fashioned

D. Toddy

**45. Which of the following drinks is stirred?**

A. Bourbon and Coke

B. Manhattan

C. Old Fashioned

D. Toddy

46. When you want twice the amount of alcohol in your mixed drink, you should ask for your drink:

A. Tall

B. Doux

C. Double

D. Down

47. Naming the bourbon you want in your glass or used in your cocktail is referred to as:

A. Well

B. Build

C. Call

D. Drop

48. Wishing people well during a special occasion is called a:

A. Toast

B. Aperitif

C. Chaser

D. Cordial

49. A fruit, flower, herb, or spice added to a drink for color is referred to as:

A. Fizz

B. Float

C. Garnish

D. Nip

50. Which of the following drinks is served without ice?

A. Neat

B. Up

C. Down

D. All of the above

51. Bourbon barrels must be made from:

A. White oak

B. Cedar

C. Cherry

D. Mesquite

52. Alcohol boils at what temperature?

A. 212 degrees Fahrenheit

B. 200 degrees Fahrenheit

C. 190 degrees Fahrenheit

D. 173 degrees Fahrenheit

53. Which Jim Beam master distiller is immortalized with a cask strength bourbon?

A. Fred Noe III

B. Booker Noe

C. Harlen Wheatley

D. Chris Morris

**54. Which master distiller helped to found the Woodford Reserve brand and launch Gentleman Jack?**

A. Harlen Wheatley

B. Chris Morris

C. Lincoln Henderson

D. Evan Williams

**55. Which master distiller is known as the "Buddha of Bourbon"?**

A. Chris Morris

B. Booker Noe

C. Jimmy Russell

D. Harlen Wheatley

**56. Which master distiller has a vodka named for him?**

A. Chris Morris

B. Booker Noe

C. Jimmy Russell

D. Harlen Wheatley

**57. Which former Four Roses master distiller later opened his own distillery?**

A. Jim Rutledge

B. Brent Elliott

C. Drew Kulsveen

D. David Pickerell

**58. Which master distiller is known as the Johnny Appleseed of distillers?**

A. Edwin Foote

B. Elmer T. Lee

C. David Pickerell

D. Brent Elliott

**59. Which master distiller is known for his wheated bourbons?**

A. Elmer T. Lee

B. Chris Morris

C. Drew Kulsveen

D. Edwin Foote

**60. Which master distiller is known as the "father of single barrel bourbon"?**

A. Elmer T. Lee

B. Chris Morris

C. Edwin Foote

D. Jimmy Russell

**61. Who is considered the "father of bourbon"?**

A. Jimmy Russell

B. Evan Williams

C. The Reverend Elijah Craig

D. Edwin Foote

62. Which Jim Beam master distiller also serves as the ambassador of the small batch line of products from that distillery?

A. Booker Noe

B. Fred Noe III

C. Brent Elliott

D. Elmer T. Lee

63. Which Willett master distiller has been nominated for a James Beard Award?

A. Harlen Wheatley

B. David Pickerell

C. Steve Nally

D. Drew Kulsveen

64. Which master distiller spent time at Maker's Mark and Bardstown Bourbon Company?

A. Drew Kulsveen

B. Steve Nally

C. David Pickerell

D. Brent Elliot

I always welcome the opportunity to learn from a living legend such as Master Distiller Jimmy Russell (right). *Photo by Kimberly Schmid*

# ACKNOWLEDGMENTS

MANY PEOPLE HELP PRODUCE A BOOK. THE IDEA that a book is written by one person without any help from others is ridiculous. I would like to thank the following people for their direct or indirect contributions to this project:

To my wife, Kimberly, for your love, support, ideas, suggestions, and copyediting, thank you!

To my sons and new daughter-in-law, Thomas and Kendall and Michael, thank you for your love and support! I can't wait to see each of you and share a little bourbon.

To my sisters and brother and their families, Gretchen, Rachel, Justin, Bennett, Ana, Shane, and John, thank you for your love and support.

To Scot Duval for your friendly counsel.

To Erin King and David Tarnoff for their advice and weekly support.

To Chris Morris and Chris Poynter from Brown-Forman for helping facilitate pictures for this project.

To Anna Hibbs and Jeff Crowe from Heaven Hill for helping facilitate pictures for this project.

To Amandalin Ryan from the Kentucky Distillers' Association and the Kentucky Bourbon Trail for helping facilitate pictures for this project.

To the master distillers who shared their knowledge, including Lincoln Henderson, Parker Beam, Jimmy Russell, Chris Morris, Fred Noe, Harlen Wheatley, and Craig Beam.

To the other writers and bourbon experts who helped me learn about bourbon: Susan Reigler, Joy Perrine, Steve Coomes, Charles "Chuck" Cowdery, Michael Veach, Maggie Kimberl, Molly Wellman, Carol Peachee, Bernie Lubbers, Peggy Noe Stevens, Julian Van Winkle III, Sara Havens, David Dominé, Clay Risen, Tim Laird, and Fred Minnick.

Finally, I would like to thank the following musical artists to whom I listened in my office as I wrote this book: Silk Sonic, Bruno Mars, Anderson .Paak, Gary Allan, the Who, Justin Timberlake, Daryl Hall, CeeLo Green, Alicia Keys, Kelly Clarkson, Sting, Shaggy, Albert Cummings, Snoop Dogg, Nathaniel Rateliff, Blues Delight, Phil Collins, Sam Smith, Jurassic 5, Maxwell, Sade, John Legend, Chris Stapleton, and Santana.

# BIBLIOGRAPHY

Amis, Kingsley. *Everyday Drinking: The Distilled Kingsley Amis*. New York: Bloomsbury, 2008.

Cowdery, Charles K. *Bourbon, Straight: The Uncut and Unfiltered Story of American Whiskey*. Chicago: Made & Bottled in Kentucky, 2004.

Minnick, Fred. *Bourbon: The Rise, Fall, and Rebirth of an American Whiskey*. Minneapolis: Voyageur, 2016.

Perrine, Joy, and Susan Reigler. *The Kentucky Bourbon Cocktail Book*. Lexington: University Press of Kentucky, 2009.

Reed, Ben. *Ben Reed's Bartender's Guide*. London: Ryland, Peters & Small, 2006.

Reigler, Susan. *Kentucky Bourbon Country: The Essential Travel Guide*. 3rd ed. Lexington: University Press of Kentucky, 2020.

Ruffenach, Linda. *How to Be a Bourbon Badass*. Bloomington, Ind.: Red Lightning Books, 2018.

Schmid, Albert W. A. *The Hot Brown*. Bloomington, Ind.: Red Lightning Books, 2017.

———. *How to Drink Like a Mobster*. Bloomington, Ind.: Red Lightning Books, 2018.

———. *How to Drink Like a Rockstar*. Bloomington, Ind.: Red Lightning Books, 2020.

———. *How to Drink Like a Royal*. Bloomington, Ind.: Red Lightning Books, 2020.

———. *How to Drink Like a Spy*. Bloomington, Ind.: Red Lightning Books, 2019.

———. *The Kentucky Bourbon Cookbook*. Lexington: University Press of Kentucky, 2010.

———. *The Manhattan Cocktail: A Modern Guide to the Whiskey Classic*. Lexington: University Press of Kentucky, 2015.

———. *The Old Fashioned: An Essential Guide to the Original Whiskey Cocktail*. Lexington: University Press of Kentucky, 2013.

Veach, Michael R. *Kentucky Bourbon Whiskey: An American Heritage*. Lexington: University Press of Kentucky, 2013.

# ANSWER KEY

A bourbon quiz appears at the end of every chapter except 5, 8, and 9, which feature "practical exams." Readers are advised to enjoy the quizzes before turning to this answer key. In other words, *no peeking!*

## QUIZ #1

1. Which of the following bourbons is considered a "classic" recipe?
**Answer: B. Elijah Craig**

2. Which of the following bourbons is considered a "wheated" bourbon?
**Answer: A. W. L. Weller**

3. Which of the following bourbons is considered a "high-rye" bourbon?
**Answer: D. Breckenridge**

4. A bourbon that is hard to find might be referred to as a:
**Answer: B. Unicorn**

5. A small batch bourbon is defined as:
**Answer: D. There is no legal definition for small batch**

6. Your tasting kit should include which of the following items?
**Answer: D. All of the above**

7. Bottled-in-bond is bottled at what proof?
**Answer: C. 100**

8. A barrel maker is referred to as a:
**Answer: C. Cooper**

9. An age statement defines what about the bourbon in the bottle?
**Answer: B. The lowest age of the whiskey**

10. What is the evaporation of whiskey in the barrel referred to as?
**Answer: B. Angel's share**

11. When tasting bourbon, smelling the bourbon is referred to as:
**Answer: A. Nosing**

12. A liquor store that sells prize bourbons at or near retail price is referred to as:
**Answer: B. Honey hole**

13. What is the most desirable part of the distillation?
**Answer: B. The hearts**

14. The rickhouse is:
**Answer: B. A warehouse where bourbon is stored**

15. The word *handcrafted* on the label:
**Answer: D. Has no legal meaning**


# QUIZ #2

1. Bourbon barrels must be made from:
**Answer: A. White Oak**

2. A barrel maker is known as a:
**Answer: A. Cooper**

3. Alcohol boils at what temperature?
**Answer: D. 173 degrees Fahrenheit**

4. Which Jim Beam master distiller is immortalized with a cask strength bourbon?
**Answer: B. Booker Noe**

5. Which master distiller helped to found the Woodford Reserve brand and launch Jack Daniel's Single Barrel?
**Answer: C. Lincoln Henderson**

6. Which master distiller is known as the "Buddha of Bourbon"?
**Answer: C. Jimmy Russell**

7. Which master distiller has a vodka named for him?
**Answer: D. Harlen Wheatley**

8. Which former Four Roses master distiller later opened his own distillery?
**Answer: A. Jim Rutledge**

9. Which master distiller is known as the Johnny Appleseed of American whiskey?
**Answer: C. David Pickerell**

10. Which master distiller is known for his wheated bourbons?
**Answer: D. Edwin Foote**

11. Which master distiller is known as the "father of single barrel bourbon"?
**Answer: A. Elmer T. Lee**

12. Who is considered the "father" of bourbon?
**Answer: C. The Reverend Elijah Craig**

13. Which Jim Beam master distiller also serves as the ambassador of the small batch line of products from that distillery?
**Answer: B. Fred Noe III**

14. Which Willett master distiller has been nominated for a James Beard Award?
**Answer: D. Drew Kulsveen**

15. Which master distiller spent time at Maker's Mark and Bardstown Bourbon Company?
**Answer: B. Steve Nally**

# QUIZ #3

1. Bourbon must be made in:
**Answer: B. The United States**

2. What city is known as the capital of bourbon?
**Answer: C. Bardstown, Kentucky**

3. The Eighteenth Amendment to the US Constitution limited all of the following except:
**Answer: D. Consumption**

4. The "proof" of a whiskey is the alcohol by volume:
**Answer: A. Doubled**

5. Before the Whiskey Rebellion, who suggested a tax on whiskey to Congress?
**Answer: B. Alexander Hamilton**

6. Who said, "I have never in my life seen a Kentuckian who didn't have a gun, a pack of cards, and a jug of whiskey"?
**Answer: C. Andrew Jackson**

7. During Prohibition organized crime made money with which of the following:
**Answer: C. Both of the above**

8. Which president drank a shot of bourbon every morning with breakfast?
**Answer: C. Harry S. Truman**

9. Which of the following amendments to the Constitution of the United States is the only one to repeal another amendment?
**Answer: D. Twenty-First**

10. According to law, what makes up most of the mash for bourbon?
**Answer: A. Corn**

11. Bourbon must be bottled at what proof minimum?
**Answer: A. 80**

12. Bourbon must be aged in which of the following?
**Answer: A. Oak container**

13. Bottled-in-bond must always be bottled at what proof?
**Answer: C. 100**

14. To be labeled "straight bourbon," the whiskey in the bottle must be aged at least:
**Answer: A. Two years**

15. Bourbon must not be distilled to more than what proof?
**Answer: D. 160**

# QUIZ #4

1. What is the first flavor that humans taste?
**Answer: A. Sweet**

2. What is the first step to tasting bourbon?
**Answer: A. See**

3. What is the last step to tasting bourbon?
**Answer: E. Savor**

4. In which step in tasting should you be able to pick out aromas like vanilla, hay, caramel, and butterscotch?
**Answer: C. Sniff**

5. A good way to detect acid is:
**Answer: B. Saliva**

6. The nose can detect and distinguish at least _____ odors.
**Answer: D. 1 trillion**

7. A darker bourbon suggests that the bourbon has been:
**Answer: A. Aged longer**

8. If evaluating more than three or four bourbons, you should:
**Answer: C. Have a spit bucket at the ready**

9. A good test to pick up the aroma of bourbon is:
**Answer: A. Use your hands**

10. When looking for the aromas in bourbon, part your:
**Answer: A. Lips**

# QUIZ #6

1. If you want a chilled bourbon served without ice, you should ask for it to be served:
**Answer: B. Up**

2. If you want a bourbon served over ice, you should ask for it served:
**Answer: C. On the rocks**

3. When a liquid is added to a spirit, it is referred to as:
**Answer: D. A mixer**

4. Which of the following drinks is muddled?
**Answer: C. Old Fashioned**

5. Which of the following drinks is stirred?
**Answer: B. Manhattan**

6. When you want twice the amount of alcohol in your mixed drink, you should ask for it:
**Answer: C. Double**

7. Naming the bourbon you want in your glass or used in your cocktail is referred to as a:
**Answer: C. Call**

8. Wishing people well during a special occasion is called:
**Answer: A. A toast**

9. A fruit, flower, herb, or spice added to a drink for color is referred to as:
**Answer: C. Garnish**

10. Which of the following refers to a drink served without ice?
**Answer: A. Neat**

# QUIZ #7

1. The Old Fashioned has which of the following?
**Answer: D. All of the above**

2. The Perfect Manhattan has which of the following?
**Answer: D. All of the above**

3. Which of the following cocktails is the official drink of the Kentucky Derby?
**Answer: B. Mint Julep**

4. Which of the following cocktails is created with a sparkling wine?
**Answer: C. Seelbach**

5. Which of the following cocktails was created at the Brown Hotel?
**Answer: B. Muhammad Ali Smash**

6. Which of the following cocktails is similar to the gin-based Negroni?
**Answer: B. Boulevardier**

7. Which of the following drinks is made with equal parts club soda and ginger ale?
**Answer: A. Presbyterian**

8. Which of the following cocktails is made with egg whites?
**Answer: C. Bourbon Sour**

9. Which of the following cocktails is made with white crème de cacao?
**Answer: C. Commodore**

10. Which of the following cocktails features mint in the recipe?
**Answer: D. All of the Above**

# FINAL EXAM

1. Which of the following bourbons is considered a "classic" recipe?
**Answer: B. Elijah Craig**

2. Which of the following bourbons is considered a "wheated" bourbon?
**Answer: A. W. L. Weller**

3. Which of the following bourbons is considered a "high-rye" bourbon?
**Answer: D. Breckenridge**

4. A bourbon that is hard to find might be referred to as a:
**Answer: B. Unicorn**

5. A small-batch bourbon is defined as:
**Answer: D. There is no legal definition for the term**

6. Your tasting kit should include which of the following items?
**Answer: D. All of the above**

7. Bottled-in-bond is bottled at what proof?
**Answer: C. 100**

8. A barrel maker is referred to as a:
**Answer: C. Cooper**

9. An age statement defines what about the bourbon in the bottle?
**Answer: B. The lowest age**

10. What is the evaporation of whiskey in the barrel referred to as?
**Answer: B. Angel's share**

11. When tasting bourbon, smelling the bourbon is referred to as:
**Answer: A. Nosing**

12. A liquor store that sells prize bourbons at or near retail price is referred to as:
**Answer: B. Honey hole**

13. What is the most desirable part of the distillation?
**Answer: B. Hearts**

14. The rickhouse is:
**Answer: B. A warehouse where bourbon is stored**

15. The word *handcrafted* on the label indicates:
**Answer: D. Nothing legally**

16. Bourbon must be made in:
**Answer: B. The United States**

17. What city is known as the "Capital of Bourbon"?
**Answer: C. Bardstown, Kentucky**

18. The Eighteenth Amendment to the United States Constitution limited all of the following except:
**Answer: D. Consumption**

19. The "proof" of a whiskey is the alcohol by volume:
**Answer: A. Doubled**

20. Before the Whiskey Rebellion, who suggested a tax on whiskey to Congress?
**Answer: B. Alexander Hamilton**

21. Who said, "I have never in my life seen a Kentuckian who didn't have a gun, a pack of cards, and a jug of whiskey"?
**Answer: C. Andrew Jackson**

22. During Prohibition organized crime made money with which of the following?
**Answer: C. Both of the above**

23. Which president drank a shot of bourbon every morning with breakfast?
**Answer: C. Harry S. Truman**

24. Which of the following amendments to the Constitution of the United States is the only one to repeal another amendment?
**Answer: D. Twenty-first**

25. According to law, what makes up most of the mash for bourbon?
**Answer: A. Corn**

26. Bourbon must be bottled at what proof minimum?
**Answer: A. 80**

27. Bourbon must be aged in which of the following?
**Answer: A. Oak container**

28. Bottled-in-bond must always be bottled at what proof?
**Answer: C. 100**

29. To be labeled "straight bourbon," the whiskey in the bottle must be aged at least:
**Answer: A. Two years**

30. Bourbon must not be distilled to more than what proof?
**Answer: D. 160**

31. What is the first flavor that humans taste?
**Answer: A. Sweet**

32. What is the first step to tasting bourbon?
**Answer: A. See**

33. What is the last step to tasting bourbon?
**Answer: E. Savor**

34. In which step in tasting should you be able to pick out aromas like vanilla, hay, caramel, and butterscotch?
**Answer: C. Sniff**

35. A good way to detect acid is:
**Answer: B. Saliva**

36. The nose can detect and distinguish at least _____ odors.
**Answer: E. 1 trillion**

37. A darker bourbon suggests that the bourbon has been:
**Answer: A. Aged longer**

38. If evaluating more than three or four bourbons, you should:
**Answer: C. Have a spit bucket at the ready**

39. A good test to pick up the aroma of bourbon is:
**Answer: A. Use your hands**

40. When looking for the aromas in bourbon, part your:
**Answer: A. Lips**

41. If you want a chilled bourbon served without ice, you should ask for your bourbon served:
**Answer: B. Up**

42. If you want a bourbon served over ice, you should ask for your bourbon served:
**Answer: C. On the rocks**

43. A liquid added to a spirit is referred to as:
**Answer: D. A mixer**

44. Which of the following drinks is muddled?
**Answer: C. Old Fashioned**

45. Which of the following drinks is stirred?
**Answer: B. Manhattan**

46. When you want twice the amount of alcohol in your mixed drink, you should ask for your drink:
**Answer: C. Double**

47. Naming the bourbon you want in your glass or used in your cocktail is referred to as:
**Answer: C. Call**

48. Wishing people well during a special occasion is called a:
**Answer: A. Toast**

49. A fruit, flower, herb, or spice added to a drink for color is referred to as:
**Answer: C. Garnish**

50. Which of the following drinks is served without ice?
**Answer: A. Neat**

51. Bourbon barrels must be made from:
**Answer: A. White oak**

52. Alcohol boils at what temperature?
**Answer: D. 173 degrees Fahrenheit**

53. Which Jim Beam master distiller is immortalized with a cask strength bourbon?
**Answer: B. Booker Noe**

54. Which master distiller helped to found the Woodford Reserve brand and launch Gentleman Jack?
**Answer: C. Lincoln Henderson**

55. Which master distiller is known as the "Buddha of Bourbon"?
**Answer: C. Jimmy Russell**

56. Which master distiller has a vodka named for him?
**Answer: D. Harlen Wheatley**

57. Which former Four Roses master distiller later opened his own distillery?
**Answer: A. Jim Rutledge**

58. Which master distiller is known as the Johnny Appleseed of distillers?
**Answer: C. David Pickerell**

59. Which master distiller is known for his wheated bourbons?
**Answer: D. Edwin Foote**

60. Which master distiller is known as the "father of single barrel bourbon"?
**Answer: A. Elmer T. Lee**

61. Who is considered the "father of bourbon"?
**Answer: C. The Reverend Elijah Craig**

62. Which Jim Beam master distiller also serves as the ambassador of the small batch line of products from that distillery?
**Answer: B. Fred Noe III**

63. Which Willett master distiller has been nominated for a James Beard Award?
**Answer: D. Drew Kulsveen**

64. Which master distiller spent time at Maker's Mark and Bardstown Bourbon Company?
**Answer: B. Steve Nally**

# INDEX